# Economics
## Learning and Instruction

South-Western Learning-and-Instruction Series

# Economics: Learning and Instructio

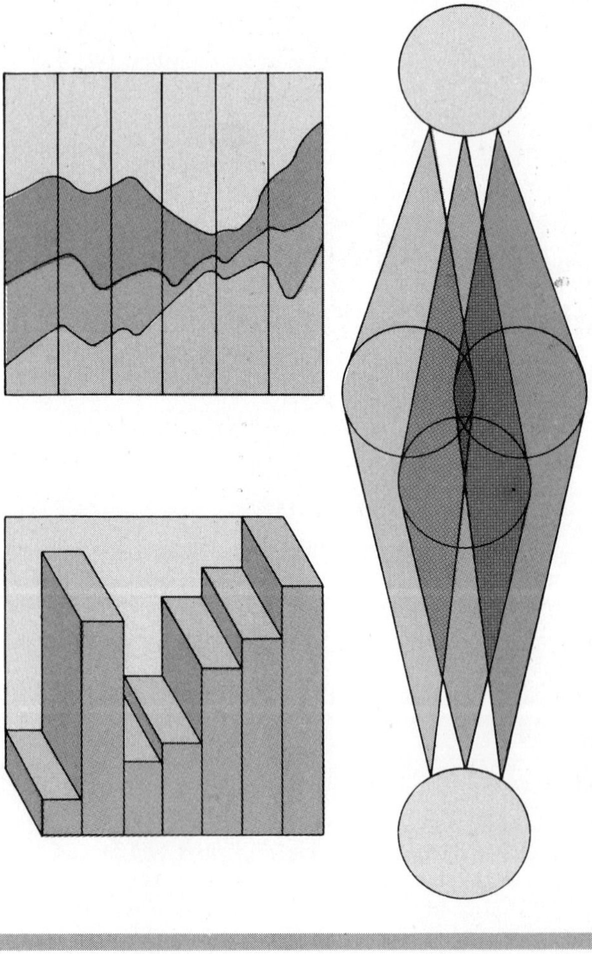

Published by
**SOUTH-WESTERN PUBLISHING CO.**
X15

CINCINNATI   WEST CHICAGO, ILL.   DALLAS   PELHAM MANOR, N.Y.   PALO ALTO, CALIF.

**Lucille G. Ford, Ph.D.**
Vice President
Dean, School of Business
   Administration/Economics
Professor of Economics
Ashland College, Ashland, Ohio

With Appreciation to
The Martha Holden Jennings Foundation

Copyright © 1982
by South-Western Publishing Co.
Cincinnati, Ohio

All Rights Reserved

The text of this publication, or any part thereof, may not be reproduced or transmitted in any form or by any means, electronic or mechanical, including photocopying, recording, storage in an information retrieval system, or otherwise, without the prior written permission of the publisher.

ISBN: 0-538-24150-0

Library of Congress Catalog Card Number: 81-83732.

1 2 3 4 5 6 D 6 5 4 3 2 1

Printed in the United States of America

# Preface

Many states acknowledge the need for elementary and secondary teachers to teach economics to achieve economic literacy in America. However, the economics instruction in the colleges and universities of the country is rarely adjusted to the nonbusiness major. It is true that economics is economics, but the education major or teacher needs to see — while studying economics — what part of the economics discipline is appropriate for teaching and how to teach that material to students. As a pioneer in economics education, the Ashland College Gill Center for Business and Economics Education received a grant from the Martha Holden Jennings Foundation of Cleveland to design an in-service and pre-service economics program, field test the program and subsequently publish a text for teachers. *ECONOMICS: Learning and Instruction* is a revision of that text.

It is difficult to properly acknowledge the many people and institutions that contributed to this document. Ideas have been shaped and reshaped from important works going back to the National Task Force Report on *Economic Education within Schools*, published in 1961, and the documents from the Developmental Economic Education Project between 1964–1969. Special recognition should be given the former President of Ashland College, Dr. Glenn L. Clayton, for his insight in creating an Ashland Center, the pioneers at Ashland in economic education, Harold Cheadle and George Tarbuck, and the staff of the Gill Center: Mrs. Ellen Keslar, Ms. Gail Hawks, Dr. Frederick Rafeld, Dr. John Fraas, Mr. Lloyd Wygant, Dr. Thomas Shockney, Mr. Jim Stephens, and Dr. Marion Blue.

June V. Gilliard, Director of Curriculum, Joint Council on Economic Education, and Diane Greene, Firestone Park Elementary, Akron City School System, graciously contributed to the elementary and secondary applications of the economic concepts. Stanley Mengel, Director of the National Center of Economic Education for Children, Lesley College; Bruce R. Daalgard, Executive Director of the Minneapolis State Council on Economic Education; and Assad El-Sobky, formerly at Ashland College, served as critique readers of earlier editions.

Several thousand in-service and pre-service teachers who received economics instruction with *ECONOMICS: Learning and Instruction* as the basic course textbook have contributed substantially to this revision. Special appreciation and recognition are due the following critique teacher readers: Christine Williams, Norma McKinley, Gaynell Cline, Christine Renner, Judy Fox, Marilyn Wright, Diana Drake, Lynette Ledbetter, Marcia Long, and especially Professor Beverly Armento of Georgia State University, as well as Assistant Field Director Hawks and Field Director Keslar of the Gill Center.

*Lucille G. Ford*

# Foreword

"The great enemy of the truth is very often not the lie — deliberate, contrived and dishonest — but the myth — persistent, persuasive and unrealistic. . . . We enjoy the comfort of opinion without the discomfort of thought."*
Economic education is a vital area of understanding not only to provide the necessary analytical tools for wise decision making at an individual level but to provide a forum for the widest possible discussion and disagreement about economic policy-making by government.

Economic literacy equips the individual to achieve levels of consumer satisfaction from limited income; to make intelligent decisions about income-earning opportunities which require individuals to know, to maintain and to improve their human capabilities; and to participate in public dialogue on crucial issues such as the amount of national, state and local taxation and the best way to spend those tax dollars.

Elementary and secondary teachers are asked to teach economics to students in the schools of this country to the end of economic literacy of Americans. Acquiring the process of economic analyses and the skills of economic reasoning is a developmental task and not achieved by packaged cures. Attention, therefore, to university level instruction for teachers was made the topic of research at Ashland College. Sixty-nine college students, sixty-nine elementary and secondary teachers and 1614 elementary and secondary students participated in this research project.

The experimental instruction method of concepts with methods is superior to a traditional textbook teaching method to increase the economic knowledge of the college student majoring in education. The usual "heavy" economics textbook teaching was found to be inferior to the focused or abstracted approach combined with methods. To understand a little economics well and instruction in methodology leads to greater economic understanding than does a presentation of refinements and details that may have the teacher confused.

From the first systematic effort to give direction and shape to economic education by the National Task Force on Economic Education in 1961, much work has been completed. For example, the substantial work of the Joint Council of Economic Education in 1964, which came to be known as DEEP (Developmental Economic Education Program), expanded and cast in operational terms the "minimal economic understanding" for every high school graduate, how this understanding might be introduced and at what grade level the material could be entered in the existing curriculum. The seven major areas of economics as identified by the Task Force were elaborated into 38 sub-divisions with an additional 118 sub-sub-divisions.

The latest framework of economics and the one with perhaps the greatest

---

*John F. Kennedy (Yale University address, 1962).

collective effort is one published by the Joint Council of Economic Education in 1977 entitled *Master Curriculum Guide in Economics for the Nation's Schools*. Part I of this work is "A Framework for Teaching Economics: Basic Concepts" and Part II is "Strategies for Teaching Economics." The goal of this work is "to fashion a more effective system increasing the economic understanding of pre-university students."* Schematic overviews are available: good concept listings are available and good textbooks are available. However, to move toward the goal of economic literacy of Americans, more reduction in volume, simplification of the "parts" is needed. An excellent inclusive concept listing may be too elaborate for a particular purpose. Also the concept list, by itself, may invite an elaborate and/or confusing presentation by the instructor. The need to limit the concept list should be followed by limiting or selecting the crucial content under the concept to be taught. The selection and confinement of relevant material to a concept area is a fundamental requirement for successful economic education.

The structure of this text is to strip away the complexities of economics by writing and teaching from eight simplified yet comprehensive economic concept areas. This simplification is the boldness of the text — a necessary and important task.

Ideally, teachers and education majors should prepare themselves to teach economics by receiving economics instruction at the University level according to the design used in this research:

$$\text{Economic Understandings} + \text{Methods of Teaching} + \text{Practice in the Classroom}$$

*ECONOMICS: Learning and Instruction* may be used by any university or college economics or education professor where instruction to teach economics at the pre-university level is desired. The linkage of economic knowledge to the application of that economic knowledge is crucial. This text is one link between the university course in economics and the teacher of economics in the elementary and secondary classrooms of our country.

---

**Master Curriculum Guide in Economics for the Nation's Schools*, Part I-A Framework for Teaching Economics: Basic Concepts. Joint Council of Economic Education, New York, 1977, p. 1.

# Table of Contents

**INTRODUCTION**     1

**BASIC ECONOMIC CONCEPT AREAS**

**Concept Area I:** *The Economic Problem and Alternative Economic Systems*     7
- Overview of Concept Area    8
- List of Economic Understandings in Concept Area    13
- Teaching Applications in Concept Area    15
  1. University Level Instruction    15
  2. Secondary Level Instruction    21
  3. Elementary Level Instruction    25
- Evaluation Instrument of Concept Area    31

**Concept Area II:** *Demand and Supply: The Market in Operation*     33
- Overview of Concept Area    34
- List of Economic Understandings in Concept Area    38
- Teaching Applications in Concept Area    39
  1. University Level Instruction    39
  2. Secondary Level Instruction    46
  3. Elementary Level Instruction    52
- Evaluation Instrument of Concept Area    56

**Concept Area III:** *Incomes: Origins and Distributions*     59
- Overview of Concept Area    60
- List of Economic Understandings in Concept Area    64
- Teaching Applications in Concept Area    65
  1. University Level Instruction    65
  2. Secondary Level Instruction    68
  3. Elementary Level Instruction    72
- Evaluation Instrument of Concept Area    74

**Concept Area IV:** *Profits, Savings and Economic Growth*     77
- Overview of Concept Area    78
- List of Economic Understandings in Concept Area    81
- Teaching Applications in Concept Area    82
  1. University Level Instruction    82
  2. Secondary Level Instruction    89
  3. Elementary Level Instruction    95
- Evaluation Instrument of Concept Area    97

**Concept Area V:** *Consumer Spending and Saving*     99
  Overview of Concept Area    100
  List of Economic Understandings in Concept Area    102
  Teaching Applications in Concept Area    103
    1. University Level Instruction    103
    2. Secondary Level Instruction    108
    3. Elementary Level Instruction    110
  Evaluation Instrument of Concept Area    114

**Concept Area VI:** *The Economic Functions of Government: Fiscal Policy*     117
  Overview of Concept Area    118
  List of Economic Understandings in Concept Area    122
  Teaching Applications in Concept Area    123
    1. University Level Instruction    123
    2. Secondary Level Instruction    128
    3. Elementary Level Instruction    132
  Evaluation Instrument of Concept Area    135

**Concept Area VII:** *Money, Monetary Policy and the Federal Reserve System*     137
  Overview of Concept Area    138
  List of Economic Understandings in Concept Area    142
  Teaching Applications in Concept Area    143
    1. University Level Instruction    143
    2. Secondary Level Instruction    148
    3. Elementary Level Instruction    151
  Evaluation Instrument of Concept Area    154

**Concept Area VIII:** *International Economics*     157
  Overview of Concept Area    158
  List of Economic Understandings in Concept Area    162
  Teaching Applications in Concept Area    163
    1. University Level Instruction    163
    2. Secondary Level Instruction    168
    3. Elementary Level Instruction    172
  Evaluation Instrument of Concept Area    173

**EPILOGUE**     174

**GLOSSARY**     176

**BIBLIOGRAPHY**     183

# INTRODUCTION

Economics has to do with scarcity — unlimited wants in conflict with limited resources. Against scarcity the economist sees the society as an elaborate mechanism to accomplish production and distribution necessary to alleviate scarcity and increase the human welfare. It is important that the economist, the student and the American public in general see this as the reason for being concerned with economics. The value of the individual and the collective economic decisions of the American people may well be measured in terms of the degree to which the welfare of the people is advanced.

The American economic mechanism is called a market system. In the American market system, the vast array of economic decisions is left to individuals, as they fill the roles of consumer, voter, worker, saver and investor. It is, therefore, impossible to grasp or understand the American economic mechanism without a knowledge of economics. Since individuals are the key decision makers in a market system, all individuals have great need to understand the way in which their decisions affect themselves and their society. Economic literacy in a market system is a large charge as well as a large challenge. The dimension of economic understanding requires two things: a mastery of economic principles and their relationship with each other and an ability to apply the principles and to learn to analyze policy issues systematically.

This text is designed to include both these dimensions for improvement of economic understanding. The structure of the text views the economic role of the individual in a market society as a three part overlapping interrelationship. These three responsibilities, which in terms of each other are both in conflict and in harmony, are:

## 2 Introduction

● **PERSONAL AND HOUSEHOLD FINANCE**
(Spending and savings program of the household.)

● **PRODUCER AND MANAGER OF PRODUCTION**
(Producer of output and consumer of that output.)

● **DIRECTOR OF PUBLIC PRODUCTION**
(Spending and saving programs—as a citizen in one's democratic role.)

Further, the three economic responsibilities of the individual are influenced by both *Scarcity* and the *Economic Goals of Society*.

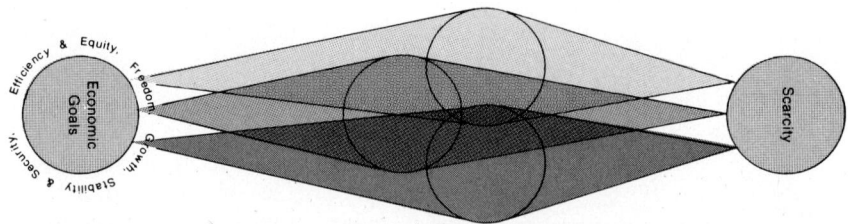

● -Personal and Household Finance (Spending and savings program of the household.)

● -Producer and Manager of Production (Producer of output and consumer of that output.)

● -Director of Public Production (Spending and saving programs—as a citizen in one's democratic role.)

A larger schematic model of these interrelationships is provided on page 6.

The crucial economics content of the text is confined to the following eight *Basic Concept Areas:*

*The Economic Problem and Alternative Economic Systems*
*Demand and Supply: The Market in Operation*
*Incomes: Origins and Distributions*
*Profits, Savings, and Economic Growth*
*Consumer Spending and Saving*
*The Economic Functions of Government: Fiscal Policy*
*Money, Monetary Policy and the Federal Reserve System*
*International Economics*

By intent, this material is concise, yet comprehensive enough to distill, abstract and reinforce for the student the important concept areas in a complex economic world. When students become teachers they need to understand, as clearly as possible, the basic economic principles or concepts from which they teach.

The inclusion of the Personal and Household Finance area is unusual by traditional standards. Neither the early Task Force Report nor the 1977 Joint Council of Economic Education Report includes this consumer role. The absence of the Consumer Role is quite understandable. Economics is not buymanship and may not belong in a basic course. Yet the use of the Consumer Role, carefully done, can be a highly acceptable vehicle for teaching economics. Young people quickly understand the consumer and/or individual role and may be led, therefore, into viewing and understanding the more complex economic responsibilities before them.

**Each Concept Area is presented with an:**

*Overview of Concept Area*

> A concise explanation of the basic concept area as well as the relationship of its components to one another.

*List of Economic Understandings in Concept Area*

> The fundamental economic observations from the economic overview.

*Teaching Applications in Concept Area*

> *University Level*
>
>> Applications of concept areas for the university level are provided for both university instructors and university students.
>
> *Secondary Level Instruction*
>
> *Elementary Level Instruction*

The pre-university level applications are presented to introduce university students to economic application examples at the elementary and secondary levels. Economics is an excellent vehicle for teaching reading and mathematics; therefore, it should be emphasized here and by university professors that economics need not add "weight" or complexity to the elementary or secondary curriculum. Rather, economics provides interesting subject matter for use while improving reading and mathematics skills. When teachers prepare their own teaching/learning units for an elementary or secondary classroom, they will want to refer to their education textbooks. For convenience, a typical teaching/learning unit is included in the bibliography of this text.

## Introduction

*Evaluation Instrument of Concept Area*

A concept area evaluation instrument concludes the concept area. The evaluation technique of any one university professor will vary with that professor. It is recommended that the evaluation instrument or test included in the text for each Concept Area be administered twice during the instruction of the Area. The first administration of the test will identify the weak areas of the students' knowledge. The second administration of the same test can be used for grading purposes. The evaluation goal is to measure understanding of the interrelationships among concept components in the area and not to focus on single economic terms or conditions in isolation. Therefore, individual application evaluations are not included. These could be developed by professors if desired. Commercially prepared tests in economics are identified in the bibliography of this text.

The text does not include a separate section on current issues because those issues change rapidly. However, the application section of Concept Areas Six, Seven, and Eight of the text do present, for example, analyses of current issues.

A most effective teaching device for economics professors is to ask students to analyze a set of current newspaper clippings that cover the basic concept areas.

Teams may be set up from a class to study one assigned issue and concept area. After the teams have concluded their study, either the team as a whole or an indicated spokesperson may report to the class for further discussion of the entire class. If professors prefer, a number of good "Readings on Economic Issues" are available commercially.

**The format of the Application examples of each Concept Area is:**

*Activity Title*

Primary Economic Understanding
Secondary Economic Understanding

*Purposes of Activity*

*Materials and Instructions for Activity*

*Economic Content and Debriefing of Activity*

The format of the application example is self-explanatory. Special consideration, however, should be given the Economic Content and Debriefing section. An activity can be good within itself; yet, fail to accomplish the purpose of economics teaching unless carefully understood.

Although each application included in the text has been classroom tested, professors at the university level or teachers in the elementary or secondary schools will want to adapt the applications to their particular situation.

University professors can conveniently assign a section of this text when the Concept Area described coincides with the material being covered in the economics textbook. It is also possible for economics professors to use it as a "basic text" for an economics course for in-service teachers or for an education majors class with supplemental readings as deemed appropriate. In any event, this text is a useful resource for university or college professors as they instruct teachers in economics and for education majors as they study economics and prepare to teach economics to students in the elementary and secondary schools of the country. Furthermore, practicing teachers with or without university level instruction in economics will find the text a valuable resource.

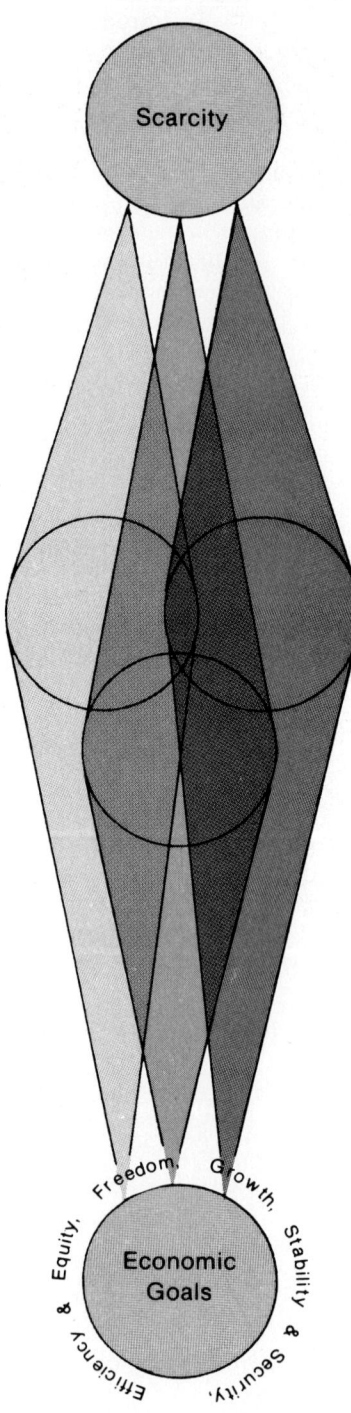

- Personal and Household Finance (Spending and savings program of the household.)

- Producer and Manager of Production (Producer of output and consumer of that output.)

- Director of Public Production (Spending and saving programs—as a citizen in one's democratic role.)

# THE ECONOMIC PROBLEM AND ALTERNATIVE ECONOMIC SYSTEMS

*Concept Area I*

## Contents

**OVERVIEW OF CONCEPT AREA 1**   8

Scarcity and Choice   8
Factors of Production   8
Opportunity Cost   8
Specialization   9
Interdependence   9
Alternative Economic Systems   9
Market System Characteristics   10
Economic Goals   12

**LIST OF ECONOMIC UNDERSTANDINGS IN CONCEPT AREA 1**   13

**TEACHING APPLICATIONS IN CONCEPT AREA 1**   15

**University Level Instruction**   15

   1. The Survival Game   15
   2. Scarcity and Allocation   18
   3. Specialization: A Simulation Game   19

**Secondary Level Instruction**   21

   1. The Ice Cream Simulation Game   21
   2. Making an Economic Decision   22
   3. Increasing Productivity   23

**Elementary Level Instruction**   25

   1. Interdependence   25
   2. Mountain of Wishes   26
   3. Opportunity Cost   27
   4. Competition and the Market System   29

**EVALUATION INSTRUMENT OF CONCEPT AREA 1**   31

# OVERVIEW OF CONCEPT AREA I

**SCARCITY AND CHOICE** Human wants exceed society's ability to satisfy them. All societies are faced with the problem of scarcity. Economics is the social science that addresses this problem, namely, which of society's wants to satisfy and which resources are to be used to satisfy these wants. Thus, it could be stated that economics is the study of the various *choices* available to satisfy one's unlimited wants with one's limited resources. Each society has to solve this allocation problem by selecting an economic system that best fits its needs and fulfills its goals and aspirations. Thus, whatever economic system chosen it must answer the following basic questions that face every society or nation:

- What and how much should be produced? (Decision Question)
- How should production take place? (Production Question)
- How should what is produced be distributed among the population? (Distribution Question)

**FACTORS OF PRODUCTION.** The satisfaction of an individual's wants is limited by that individual's income; which, in turn, is limited by the resources that the individual controls. Individuals have control over their own labor and other resources that they might own. Like the individual, society's resources are also limited and thus its ability to satisfy its wants is limited by the resources that it controls. A society's resources are usually referred to as *factors of production* and are classified as *land, labor, capital,* and *entrepreneurship. Land* is any resource that is a gift of nature, this includes minerals, agricultural land, water, etc. *Labor* is the productive services available to that society from its population in terms of hours of work. *Capital* is society's past savings that have been transformed into man-made products that are used in the production of other goods. This includes machines, trucks, tools, etc. Finally, *entrepreneurship* is the ability to assemble the other three factors of production, (land, labor and capital) and produce a good or service that society deems useful for satisfying one of its unlimited wants.

**OPPORTUNITY COST.** Every time an individual, a household or society as a whole, makes a particular choice to satisfy a particular want, it is forgoing the opportunity to satisfy another want. Therefore, the cost of satisfying this want is the value of the next best opportunity open to the user of a resource or a spender of money. In such choices the individual or the group is trading off less of one thing for more of something else. This is the cost of making a choice which economists refer to as *opportunity cost*. Basically, this involves comparing the various costs and benefits of each alternative choice. This concept makes it possible to evaluate all the costs of making a particular economic decision in a comprehensive fashion.

**SPECIALIZATION.** Taking advantage of greater efficiency will release some productive resources for other uses. Society has been able to increase its output of goods and services with the same or fewer resources by means of specialization, mechanization, and human capital. The production process may be divided by region or by job: production in each region will be specialized according to advantages it has for using resources efficiently, and the worker, therefore, is more productive as a result of performing repetitive tasks or having special capabilities. Mechanization is the use of capital goods to increase the productivity of labor. Human capital increases the productivity of the labor resource by training and education. All of these techniques allow each factor of production to yield its greatest possible amount of society's wants.

Since resources are scarce relative to human wants, the most efficient use of resources would lead to the satisfaction of the greatest amount of wants.

**INTERDEPENDENCE.** Partly due to specialization, the production of goods and services is a complicated matter that requires a complex economic system. The increase in specialization, division of labor and mechanization has resulted in increased *interdependence* as each household within the system finds itself more and more dependent on the whole economic system for the goods and services that they consume. As a result of that interdependence, our economic lives have become very complex. No one household, community or even large city can claim self-sufficiency, but rather, each is in part specialized in the activity that gives it the greatest advantage. Trade among economic units then allows the satisfaction of economic wants.

**ALTERNATIVE ECONOMIC SYSTEMS.** In general, there are three alternative ways to answer the basic economic questions of production and distribution. (Economic systems differ according to . . . who makes the basic economic decisions in response to the basic questions of production and distribution.) First, there is the economic system organized by the rules of *tradition*—rules of custom and habit sanctioned by long usage. The problems of choice, production and distribution are solved by utilizing almost exclusively social institutions established by past generations. This kind of system has a clearly defined role for every individual in the society determined at birth. Members of such societies traded goods or bought and sold services; but they did not buy or sell the elements that entered into production of these goods and services. Nor, did they entrust the distribution of the output primarily to a marketplace. Typically, the solution imposed by tradition is a static one in which little change occurs over long periods of time. An example of such a system is found in the caste system of India and some of the tribal societies of Africa and the Middle East. Some elements of tradition exist in a command and market system.

Second, there is the *command* economic system that solves the three economic problems by directing the allocation of resources through a central governmental authority, usually the dominant political party. In such a system the government role can be one of an extreme totalitarian nature or one of a more democratic form. Under the command system the central authority not only owns most of the resources but also directs their allocation according to its own set of established priorities which may differ from the typical consumer's priorities. In the command system the production of capital goods is usually given a much higher priority than the production of consumer goods and services; this emphasis tends to result in more rapid economic growth. Examples of the command system can be found in the Soviet Union, China, Yugoslavia and most other communist countries.

Finally, the *market* system solves the three basic questions by allowing the society to insure its own provisioning with a minimum of recourse to either tradition or command. The fundamental relationship of production and distribution in a market system is often presented graphically as shown on the following page.

**MARKET SYSTEM CHARACTERISTICS.** The market system is based on the *private ownership* of society's resources. It is the *consumer* therefore, who is the primary *director* of the economy. The consumer is sovereign not as an individual but as a member of an entire society which collectively guides and controls its productive effort through a market mechanism. Through personal decisions the individual determines the composition of the output of goods and services to be produced. These decisions, together with the cost of production, determine the price of these goods and services. Prices, in turn, play a large part in answering the basic economic questions. The *motivation* behind the market system is *profit*, (the drive to maximize one's income while minimizing one's ex-

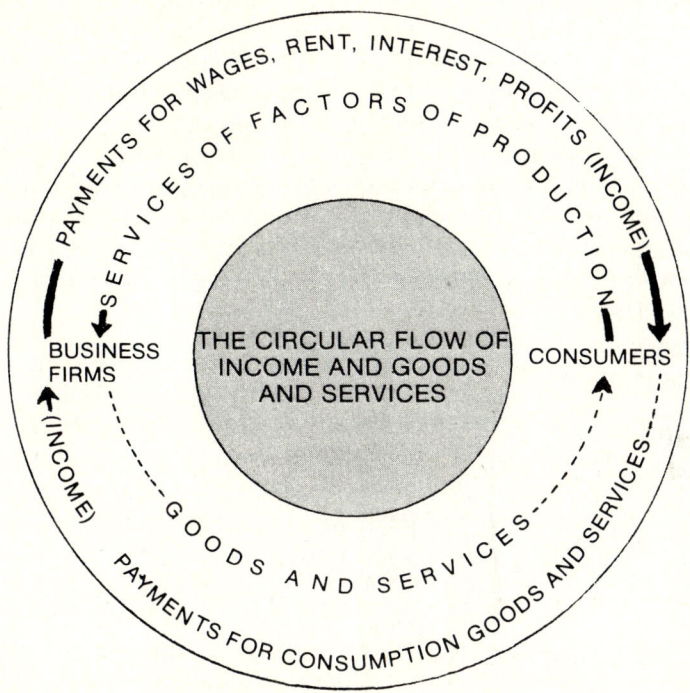

penditures). Through individual pursuit of profit or gain an efficient and complex mode of organizing society emerges from a seemingly uncontrolled situation. The automatic or built-in *regulator* of the market system is *competition*. Competition contains the economic drive by pitting seller against seller and buyer against buyer. This is true in the market for goods and services and the market for resources.

To better understand the operation of a pure or free market system, imagine that people want more bicycles and the supply is very limited. People would be willing to pay more—and the price of bicycles would rise. Making and selling bicycles would become more profitable and more companies would go into business. They would be able to pay high wages and therefore, could attract workers away from less profitable industries. Workers sell their labor and want the highest price possible. The makers of bicycles would also be able to pay higher prices for machinery and higher interest for loans. So the output of bicycles would increase because the bicycle makers were able to bid workers, money, and machines away from less profitable industries, ones that made things people didn't want so much.

In the case of two bicycle producers where one firm has lower costs and is more efficient than the other, the efficient firm could eventually put the inefficient one out of business. Free prices and higher wages also reward good workers and provide an incentive for them to do their best.*

The American Economic system is best described as a market system with a *special* role assigned to *government*. That is why it is usually referred to as a mixed economy and not a pure or free market economy. In the United States approximately thirty-three percent of the goods and services are produced by the private sector for the government. Many Western European economies are socialistic and thus allow a larger role to be played by government than does the United States. In most of these European countries the government produces goods and services alongside their private market sector.

**ECONOMIC GOALS.** The people of any economic system should choose a set of *economic goals* that are compatible with their social and political aspirations. The U.S. economy has traditionally directed itself towards a particular set of goals which includes *economic freedom, economic growth, economic stability and security, economic efficiency,* and *equity. Economic freedom* deals with the right of individuals to make their own economic decisions (where to work and how to spend their income) as long as they remain within the law. *Economic growth* is the condition of a rising standard of living for the individual; a greater per capita output of goods and services. Without economic growth little opportunity would be available for the youth who are entering the labor force. *Economic stability and security* guarantee the people a high level of employment without inflation and at the same time provide a mechanism for the individual who cannot fit in the system to maintain a minimum level of subsistence. *Economic efficiency* is the result of the utilization of the economy's scarce resources in their best possible use while *economic equity* instills an element of fairness (as the society sees it) in this process.

---

*Adapted from *The Price System,* Economic Education Series, Federal Reserve Bank of Philadelphia, Pa.

# LIST OF ECONOMIC UNDERSTANDINGS IN CONCEPT AREA 1

1. Economics is a study of the efforts of human societies to utilize limited resources to satisfy unlimited wants.

2. The basic questions any economic system must answer are:

   What and how much is to be produced?
   How should production take place?
   How should what is produced be distributed among the population?

3. A society's ability to satisfy its wants is limited by the factors of production (land, labor, capital, and entrepreneurship) that it controls.

4. Opportunity cost is measured by the value of the best alternative use for any resource.

5. Efficiency is the ability to produce the desired effect with a minimum of effort, expense or work. Efficiency in utilization of resources results in a higher standard of living.

6. Efficiency in production is achieved through division of labor, specialization and the mechanization of production.

7. Interdependence is a result of the increased use of specialization, division of labor and mechanization in production.

8. There are three basic economic systems defined to solve the problems of choice, production and distribution. They are:

   The tradition economy
   The command economy
   The market economy

9. The pure market system is characterized by the following: (a) The elevation of the individual, en masse, to a position of economic control. (Director of the System), (b) A widespread competition among all individuals in their economic activities. (Regulator of the System), and (c) The appearance of the "profit motive" as a guide for economic behavior. (Motivator of the System)

## 14   The Economic Problem and Alternative Economic Systems

10. The American Economic System is a market system with a special role assigned to government, i.e., a mixed economy.

11. Every economic system should choose a set of goals that is compatible with its people's social and political aspirations. These goals may be in conflict with each other. Economics is useful in identifying, measuring and helping to determine the choices to be made when faced with the conflicts.

# TEACHING APPLICATIONS IN CONCEPT AREA 1

## University Level Instruction

### Practice with Concept

- When was the last time you faced the universal economic problem of *scarcity*? Identify your problem, choices, the nature of scarcity, your choice, your opportunity cost.
- Identify community examples which illustrate the concept of opportunity cost.
- Give examples of regional and occupational specialization; explain how this tendency to specialize influences trade and interdependence.
- Suppose you received a wage of $200 a week for your labor. Use the circular flow model to explain how you, your employer, your income, and your needs fit into the concept of a market economy.
- Find examples in the news (local, national, or international) which illustrate the economic values of growth, security, stability, efficiency, equity and freedom. What conflicts do you see?

### The Survival Game

The student will be able to understand that:

> *Primary Economic Understanding:* Both society and the individual are faced with the decision of how to allocate their scarce resources to satisfy as many as possible of their unlimited wants.
>
> *Secondary Economic Understandings:* The opportunity cost of a resource is the best alternative use for that resource.

*Purpose:* This simulation presents a situation in which students as individuals must make a choice. Their survival depends on the choice made. Once the student realizes that individuals are constantly faced with this kind of decision in their daily lives, the task of expanding the simulation to the whole society becomes an easy one.

*Materials and Instruction:* The following game should be reproduced and handed to each student to read and select the items they will take on the survival trek keeping in mind the 50 lb. weight limitation.

# 16   The Economic Problem and Alternative Economic Systems

## OUTDOOR ENDURANCE*

Imagine that a friend stops by your house on a Saturday morning in October and suggests that you go with him for a day-long drive in the mountains to try out his new jeep. You quickly pull on jeans, a t-shirt and sneakers and go along. By late afternoon you are on a trail in a remote part of the Rockies, when suddenly a snow storm blows up. The trail soon becomes almost impassable and you can hardly see where you are going. Suddenly the jeep starts to skid and you plunge several hundred feet down a steep mountainside. Your friend is killed instantly and the jeep is completely wrecked, but fortunately you have only a few scratches. By your best estimate you are thirty to forty miles from the nearest source of help. Luckily you discover a summer cabin nearby. Although it has no heat, except a wood burning fireplace, and no telephone, it does offer shelter and about a week's supply of food. You soon realize that you cannot hope to stay in the cabin until you are rescued, for no one has any idea where to start looking for you. Therefore, when the storm starts to abate, leaving almost three feet of dry powder snow, you decide to try to follow the trail back to civilization. You are fortunate that the cabin is well stocked with camping equipment and other supplies and you can take almost anything you want, but you know that your survival over the three days it will probably take you to reach help will depend partly on how carefully you select what equipment to take. Continued on page 17 are listed some of the materials the cabin contains and their weight. Decide which of the items you will wear or carry, not to exceed a total of 50 pounds.

*Economic Content and Debriefing:*

1. The 50 pound weight limitation represents the individual's limited resources, whereas survival represents unlimited wants.

2. All individuals must make a choice with regards to which of their unlimited wants they will satisfy with their limited resources.

3. Each student will be able to compare his/her choices with the choices of other students in the class and with the choices of an expert mountain climber (see Key). Have students explain their choices in terms of anticipated needs and alternative uses for scarce resources.

4. Each society has to make the same kind of choices that the individual has to make, because societies also have limited resources and unlimited wants. This is a good point to introduce the idea of opportunity cost to

---

*Outdoor Endurance Exercise* by Stanford, G., and Roark, A. *Human Interaction in Education.* Boston: Allyn & Bacon, 1974.

## The Economic Problem and Alternative Economic Systems   17

the student. Opportunity cost is the cost that the individual or society has to bear when a choice is made. The opportunity cost of choosing to take heavy woolen mittens (2 lb.) on the trek is the forgone opportunity to take a plastic canteen filled with water (2 lb.). The concept of opportunity cost clarifies to the individual and to society the consequences of making a choice, in that every want that is satisfied means that another want will have to go unsatisfied.

A. _____ wool hat (1 lb.)
B. _____ heavy wool mittens (2 lb.)
C. _____ axe (8 lb.)
D. _____ 50 feet of ⅛" rope (1 lb.)
E. _____ saucepan for melting snow for drinking (3 lb.)
F. _____ folding camping saw (1 lb.)
G. _____ rock-climbing gear, including rock hammer, pitons (10 lb.)
H. _____ 150 feet of 7/16" rope (8 lb.)
I. _____ gasoline camp stove and fuel (10 lb.)
J. _____ plastic canteen filled with water (2 lb.)
K. _____ one large can of beef stew (10 lb.)
L. _____ fire-starting kit, including matches (½ lb.)
M. _____ heavy wool jacket with hood (10 lbs.)
N. _____ pack frame and bag (6 lb.)
O. _____ five two-pound cans of soup and vegetables (10 lb.)
P. _____ sleeping bag (5 lb.)
Q. _____ downhill skis, bindings, poles (10 lb.)
R. _____ air mattress (3 lb.)
S. _____ down-filled jacket without hood (3 lb.)
T. _____ high-top hunting boots (6 lb.)
U. _____ snowshoes (5 lb.)
V. _____ canvas tent (15 lb.)
W. _____ plastic tarp (2 lb.)
X. _____ eight boxes of high protein dry cereal (4 lb. total)
Y. _____ first-aid kit with splints, and other equipment for setting bones (4 lb.)
Z. _____ first-aid kit without splints, etc. (1 lb.)
AA. _____ heavy wool pants (4 lb.)
BB. _____ knife with can opener (½ lb.)

*Key:*  
| | A | E | L | R | U | Z |
|---|---|---|---|---|---|---|
| | B | F | N | S | W | AA |
| | D | J | P | T | X | BB |

## Scarcity and Allocation*

The student will be able to understand that:

> *Primary Economic Understanding:* Every society has to face the three questions of:
> 
> (1) What and how much is to be produced?
> (2) How should production take place?
> (3) How should what is produced be distributed among the population?
> 
> Each society has to answer these questions in some manner in order to become viable.
> 
> *Secondary Economic Understanding:* The way that each society answers these questions determines its future and the standard of living of its members.

*Purpose:* In this simulation the student is placed on a deserted island and is confronted with the basic economic questions that all economies must answer. As students choose different ways to answer the questions they will be able to achieve different levels of economic prosperity (in this simulation measured in hours).

*Materials and Instructions:* This is a commercially produced game and could be purchased from the publisher. Each set includes: student instructions, fact sheets, work sheets, and a teaching manual. The fact sheets include the hourly requirements for building tools and obtaining a daily food supply. The worksheets are set so that the student starts each time period within 12 hours plus the net hours saved from previous time periods. Each period is outlined in a clear fashion so that the student can make various choices and calculate the results.

*Economic Content and Debriefing:*

1. All students or group of students will establish a separate island economy where they will be able to answer the questions of "what to produce" and "how to produce." The "for whom to produce" question is not asked in this simulation, however, it could be used as the element for tying the simulation to the more complicated real world. This could be done by posing the question itself to the class and eliciting answers on how output is distributed in the U.S. economy.

---

*Scarcity and Allocation: An Economic Decision Game* by Erwin Rausch, Diadactic Systems, Inc., Cranford, N.J. 1968.

2. Each student or group of students will make different decisions in response to the demands of survival on the island. For example, some will allocate a larger proportion of their time to the building of tools than others. Those groups will end up with a larger total amount of hours available at the end of the simulation and thus a higher standard of living. This explains the importance of the answer to the question of what to produce, that all economies face. The greater the amount of resources allocated to the production of tools the better will the economy be able to satisfy future consumption. Many other alternative decisions may be made by students relative to all three basic economic questions.

**Specialization: A Simulation Game***

The student will be able to understand that:

> *Primary Economic Understanding:* The more efficient a society is in its production process, the more output it will have available for consumption.
>
> *Secondary Economic Understanding:* Efficiency in production could be achieved through specialization, division of labor and the mechanization of production.

The use of capital equipment will increase the productivity of labor and thus the wage rate of workers.

*Purpose:* Through this simulation students will be able to see that when individuals work alone and perform all the necessary steps to produce a paper booklet the average output will be lower than if each person specialized and performed one particular task. Finally, when a stapler (the machine) is introduced into the game, output will increase even further.

*Materials and Instructions:*
This simulation requires:
One hundred or more sheets of used 8½" by 11" paper, five boxes of paper clips, and five staplers. The instructions are:

1. The class should be divided into groups (factories) of five.
2. Each factory is instructed that the objective is to make as many paper booklets as it can. A paper booklet is made by tearing a sheet of paper into four quarters and attaching them together

---

*John W. Fraas, "Specialization: A Simulation Game". *The Ohio Council for Social Studies Review*, vol. 14, no. 1, Spring 1978.

## 20  The Economic Problem and Alternative Economic Systems

   with a paper clip. A letter (A for the first group, B for the second group, etc.) is placed on the cover.
3. The students are given two minutes to construct as many booklets as possible. The students within each group must work independently (no specialization) of fellow workers. Each student working individually tears the paper, attaches the paper clip, and letters the booklet. Each worker is paid $4 per hour. Each time period is an hour.
4. The teacher records the number of booklets produced by each group.
5. The students calculate the labor cost per booklet. For example, if Group A, which consisted of five students produced 20 booklets, the labor cost per booklet would be 5 (students) x $4.00 = $20.00 ÷ 20 (booklets) = $1.00 per booklet.
6. The students are instructed to make booklets again but this time they can work as a group, i.e., one student can tear, another can paper clip the booklets, etc.
7. Steps "4" and "5" are repeated for this round's data.
8. Step "6" is repeated except staplers, which are a capital good, are to be used. Labor has increased their wages by $1 an hour for this round.
9. Steps "4" and "5" are repeated. Ask: Compare the role of workers, the total output and the unit costs of production for each phase of the game. Explain the differences.

*Economic Content and Debriefing:*

1. Students learn that total production or output of a country determines the standard of living of its people. Further, that improvement in that standard of living (assuming no change in population) can be increased only by increased production.

2. The value of specialization (increased output) is demonstrated by the activity.

3. It is recognized that increased output is possible through the combination of machines or tools with labor. Discuss "real world" examples which are analogous to this game. Evaluate the pros and cons of specialization/mechanization.

## Secondary Level Instruction

**The Ice Cream Simulation Game:**

The student will be able to understand that:

> *Primary Economic Understanding:* There are three alternative economic systems to answer the three economic questions that face a society. They are: the tradition, the command, and the market economies.

*Purpose:* This simulation will show the student how the three different systems answer the question of "how should what is produced be distributed among the population". It ignores the first two questions of "What should be produced?" and "How should it be produced?" however, it gives the teacher the opportunity to introduce these questions to the classroom for discussion at the end of the activity.

*Materials and Instruction:* Students should be asked to assume they are members of a society where age is accepted as the measure of one's importance. Use a smaller number of ice cream cones than there are students in the classroom. The instructor will ask the students the following two questions:

> How many of you would like to have an ice cream cone?
> How are we going to decide who will get the ice cream?

*Economic Content and Debriefing:*

1. The students will find that there are only three alternative ways to distribute the ice cream.

> *Alternative 1:* The ice cream is distributed to the oldest students or those students with some special status. This would be the *tradition* economic system where status sets the standard for distribution of the output of society.
>
> *Alternative 2:* The ice cream distribution is determined by the teacher. This is an example of the *command* society where an arbitrary authority determines the distribution of output.
>
> *Alternative 3:* The ice cream would be distributed by having each student bid for each ice cream cone, with the cones going to the highest bidders. (Substitute or "play" money may be used representing their weekly allowance) This would be the example of the *market* economy.

## 22   The Economic Problem and Alternative Economic Systems

2. The difference among the three economic systems could be expanded to answer the other two basic economic questions. For example, for "what is to be produced?" the students would find the three systems provide three different answers. The tradition economy would use customs and habits; the command economy would use the power of the arbitrary authority; and the market economy would use the preferences of the population to determine the composition of output.

3. The question of how to produce could be handled in the same way. In the traditional economy it is answered through customs and predetermined habits that are handed down through each generation. The command economy utilizes a production technique that is compatible with its political ideology. This may or may not be the most efficient technique of production.

**Making an Economic Decision**

The student will be able to understand that:

> *Primary Economic Understanding:* Opportunity cost is the cost of satisfying a particular want through the use of a scarce resource. It is measured by the best alternative use for that resource.
>
> *Secondary Economic Understanding:* Making an economic decision involves defining the problem, analyzing the consequences, considering the alternatives in light of the individual's goals and values and then choosing the solution.

*Purpose:* This activity is designed to emphasize to the student the concept of opportunity cost in economic decision making.

*Materials and Instructions:*

1. Compose situation cards that are relevant for applying the above concept area. *Examples:*

    a. You are 15 years old and have been doing odd jobs to earn money to buy a stereo. You have saved $150.00 and you need $300.00. A friend offers to lend you the money if you will let him use the set whenever he wishes. Will you keep saving until you have enough money of your own or take him up on his deal? How did you make your decision?
    b.  You have been babysitting to earn money for records or clothes. You have $75.00. School starts in four weeks. A

## The Economic Problem and Alternative Economic Systems

friend comes to you and says that she is in trouble and must have $50.00 immediately. She does not know when she can pay you back. Will you loan her the money? Will you buy your school clothes or records? How did you decide?

c. Your friends are all going to the Rolling Stones concert and want you to go along. You have only enough money to go but you were planning on buying an album with that money. Will you go to the concert with your friends or buy the album? How did you decide?

2. Have each student choose two cards and read them.
3. Each student should then follow the procedure of defining the problem, analyzing the consequences, consider the alternatives, with respect to their values and goals and then finally choosing a solution and identifying the opportunity cost.

*Economic Content and Debriefing:*

1. To make a sound economic decision the individual has to look at the various possible alternatives before selecting a course of action.

2. The cost of any economic decision is the alternative options that were forgone.

### Increasing Productivity

The student will understand that

*Primary Economic Understanding:* Efficiency is the ability to produce the desired effect with a minimum of effort, expense or work.

*Secondary Economic Understanding:* Efficiency (increased productivity) is achieved through use of improved technology in production.

*Purpose:* This activity provides younger students with a concrete example of the effects of improved technology on productivity.

*Materials and Instructions:*

1. Give students ten arithmetic problems similar to those shown

## 24    The Economic Problem and Alternative Economic Systems

below. Instruct them that they will be given 2 minutes in which to work the problems.

(1)  35/10535

(2)  323/1689.29

(3)  1183
     - 967

(4)  1056
     x  87

(5)  25
     x25

(6)  28
     153
     697
     1569

(7)  12.23
     7.51
     3.08
     27.96

(8)  386
     x297

(9)  702
     -599

(10) 1693
     5827
     8558
     7767

2. After 2 minutes instruct students to stop. Have them check their answers. These are as follows: (1) 301; (2) 5.23; (3) 216 (4) 92,872; (5) 625; (6) 2447; (7) 50.78; (8) 114,642; (9) 103; (10) 23,845.
3. Ask: How many had at least ten correct? 9? 8? Continue until you reach a number that represents approximately one-half of the group.
4. Ask: How do you think the productivity of this group might be improved? (If suggestions do not include use of a hand calculator, you should ask if this might improve performances.)
5. Ask for a volunteer or select one student from the group for purposes of demonstration. Ascertain the number of problems the student solved and calculate the average time taken for working one problem. After this is done give the student a hand calculator and allow him/her two minutes to work the problems. (You may wish to allow the student time to become familiar with the calculator.)

## The Economic Problem and Alternative Economic Systems

6. At the end of the 2 minutes, have the class calculate the average time taken in working one problem and to compare this with the student's prior performance. (It should be noted that there are several possible outcomes other than an increase in productivity. There may be no change or even a decrease).
7. Have students discuss and suggest the reasons for the results of the demonstration. If there was an increase students will easily identify this as resulting from the introduction of the calculator. In the case of a decrease or no change, students should suggest that with proper training or increased practice in the use of the calculator, performance (productivity) should improve.

*Economic Content and Debriefing:*

1. Ask students if a person owned a business that required workers to calculate a lot of arithmetic problems, which method would be more efficient? What effect would the introduction of the calculator have on the productivity of individual workers? If productivity increased, what effect would this have on the business firm?

2. The follow up discussion should emphasize that improved technology helps people accomplish more work in the same amount of time. This in turn enables the business firm to provide goods or services for more people.

## Elementary Level Instruction

**Interdependence**

The student will be able to understand that:

*Primary Economic Understanding:* Interdependence is a result of the increased use of specialization, the division of labor, mechanization of production, and human capital.

*Secondary Economic Understanding:* Economic interdependence allows for a larger output and, as a result, a higher standard of living.

*Purpose:* This activity is designed to show the elementary student that in today's world people are dependent on each other to satisfy their economic wants.

*Materials and Instructions:*

1. This activity is in parallel with curriculum development. At the lower level, children can relate to interdependence in the home, then, the school, community, region and the world at the upper levels.
2. Survey some magazines for pictures of people working together.
3. Students will write or verbally explain the purpose of interdependence.

*Economic Content and Debriefing:*

1. People depend on each other to combine resources for producing goods and services that satisfy wants.

2. The pictures may be arranged in a "time-line" to demonstrate growth.

3. The steps in the development of the story in the time-line are the activities that describe the stages in growth for the individual and for the economy. Interdependence facilitates this growth.

**Mountain of Wishes***

The student will be able to understand that:

*Primary Economic Understanding:* Because of scarcity of economic goods and services, a consumer must make a decision for what to consume.

*Secondary Economic Understanding:* For decision-making the consumer will list his wants in order of priority for the satisfactions that these wants can give. Achieving these satisfactions (wants) will be limited by the income of the person (allowance, gift, job, etc.)

This activity may be varied for lower and elementary levels according to the number and sophistication of variables, such as similarities, differences, needs and wants, goods and services, economic and non-economic wants, facts and fantasy.

*Purpose:* To apply categorizing of economic wants to their curriculum. Introduce and develop individual decision-making skills with consideration for the limitations of resources for satisfying their individual wants.

---

*Mountain of Wishes* from *The Child's World of Choices,* Davison & Kilgore, 1973. Reprinted by permission.

# The Economic Problem and Alternative Economic Systems

*Materials and Instruction:* Children or teacher may cut paper in the shape of rocks (or pictures from magazines). On each rock write (or paste a picture) a wish. For appropriate grade levels write the price of the goods or service.

1. Group the "wants" on a table or bulletin board to resemble a mountain.
2. Sort the wishes in the mountain according to instructions suitable at the grade level: non-economic wants and economic wants that have prices, free goods and economic goods, real goods and fantasy goods, goods and services, wants and needs.
3. Save the rocks for economic goods and services; set aside all others.
4. Give students an "income" with play money. A store may be used to sell rock "wants."
5. Each student will arrange the economic goods and services in priority order.
6. In accordance with the prices on the economics goods and services determine how many of the wants can be satisfied with the limited income.
7. Identify the goods and services that cannot be satisfied.

*Economic Content and Debriefing:*

1. Students recognize their unlimited wants and the necessity for making choices which reinforces that skill.
2. Students recognize values when they must make choices; as a result they are motivated to evaluate their decisions in terms of satisfactions.
3. Students practice matching money with goods and services for emphasizing limitations for satisfying wants.
4. Students identify the content of economics by categorizing the economic goods and services.
5. Identify the goods and services that cannot be satisfied as opportunity costs for being able to have the other goods and services.

**Opportunity Cost***

The student will be able to understand that:

> *Primary Economic Understanding:* Because resources are scarce relative to human wants, individuals, families, and the society as a whole must make choices. For every choice made there is an opportunity cost.

---

*Adapted from *Master Curriculum Guide in Economics for the Nation's Schools, Part II: Strategies for Teaching Economics, Primary Level,* Joint Council on Economic Education, New York, 1977 p. 22.

## 28    The Economic Problem and Alternative Economic Systems

*Secondary Economic Understanding:* The opportunity cost of a decision to use a resource for a particular purpose is the best alternative use for that resource.

*Purpose:* In this activity students are presented several situations in which they identify opportunities lost and gained in choosing one alternative over another. The activity also illustrates the importance of applying the concept of opportunity cost in personal and social decision making.

*Materials and Instructions:*

1. Present students with several decision making situations similar to those provided in the examples below:
   a. A family wants to get a pet. They can have only one. They live in an apartment house in the city. Which would be a better pet—a tropical fish or a dog?
   b. Susan has five dollars. She must decide whether to buy a wagon that she wants or a nice birthday gift for her mother (the price of each is $5.00). Which should Susan buy?
   c. Tom lives alone with his father on an isolated island. His parents gave him money to buy a toy. He wants a kite and a yo yo, but he only has enough money to buy one of these. Which toy should Tom buy?
   d. Debbie has been saving her money to buy a record player. She only needs $5.00 more. On Saturday Debbie could go on a picnic with her friends or she can earn $5.00 for babysitting. What would be the best choice for Debbie?
2. Have students give positive reasons for selecting each of the paired items. List all responses on the chalkboard.
3. For each of the problem situations discussed, ask students: What do you think would be the best choice? What would you gain by making this choice? What would you lose?

*Economic Content and Debriefing:*

1. The class discussion should reinforce the idea that resources are limited. It should also lead to students' understanding that once a resource is used in a certain way it is no longer available for other purposes; thus it is important that an individual, a family, or the society as a whole carefully consider the alternatives available to it. It is important to consider not only what will be gained by choosing one alternative

over another, but also, what will be lost (i.e., the opportunities foregone).

2. Have individual students share with the class a decision they had to make recently (or one that must be made in the near future). Have the class discuss the opportunities lost and gained as a result of choosing one alternative over another.

3. To expand the opportunity cost concept to the societal level, present several problems to students involving conflict over the use of resources in the local community (e.g., use of tax revenues for improving recreational facilities *vs.* a day-care center; use of city property for a park *vs.* a municipal parking lot, etc.). Have students identify alternative uses of the particular resource involved and the opportunity cost for choosing one alternative over another.

**Competition and the Market System***

The student will understand that:

> *Primary Economic Understanding:* The automatic or built-in regulator of the market system is competition.
>
> The American Economic system is a market system with a special role assigned to government.
>
> *Secondary Economic Understanding:* Economic freedom (i.e., the right of individuals to make their own economic decisions) is a major goal of the American Economic System.
>
> Economic freedom, like political freedom, is not absolute. It is limited by certain economic and legal circumstances.

*Purpose:* This activity is designed to help students understand the role of competition in the American Economic System and why government sometimes intervenes to assure competition in the marketplace. It also provides an illustration of the economic freedom exercised by individuals in the system as they pursue their own personal economic goals.

*Materials and Instructions*

1. Have several students dramatize the following story for the rest of the class.
   a. Mr. Smith and Mrs. Brown are both bakers. They have bakeries in the same community and compete against one another for business.

---

*Adapted from *Economic Education for Washington Schools, K-6,* Joint Council on Economic Education.

30   The Economic Problem and Alternative Economic Systems

  b. Mrs. Brown advertises several fancy kinds of bread.
  c. Mr. Smith puts up a sign advertising bread 2¢ a loaf cheaper than Mrs. Brown's bread.
  d. Mrs. Brown gets a new mixing machine, now she can make bread even cheaper. She now reduces the price for a loaf of bread by 4¢.
  e. Mr. Smith puts in new display cases and wraps the bread in plastic bags so it will not get stale.
  f. One day Mrs. Brown has an idea. She tells her idea to Mr. Smith. The next day the signs in both bakeries say the same price. It is 10¢ higher than it was before.

2. After the dramatization have students discuss the following: (a) What was Mrs. Brown's idea? (b) How did the bakers compete? (c) What happened to the price the consumers paid for bread when the bakers were competing? (d) Did competition make the bakers more efficient? (e) Why did the bakers agree on a price to charge for their bread? (f) What difference does it make to the consumers when producers agree on a price? (g) Why does government prevent price agreements between producers?

*Economic Content and Debriefing*

1. Business firms trying to sell similar products to the consumer are competing with one another for the consumer dollar. A firm tries to get the consumer dollar by offering goods at a lower price or by making them of a better quality than the goods sold by competing firms.

2. Competition between firms encourages producers to invent better products or more efficient ways of producing or selling them.

3. The consumer benefits from competition between firms because prices of goods are lower, the quality of goods is better, and new kinds of goods are invented.

4. The government imposes some limitations on our economic freedom in the interest of all of us (e.g., business firms cannot use false advertising or agree with other firms to fix prices).

# EVALUATION OF CONCEPT AREA I

1. Name and describe the operation of the three usually recognized economic systems in terms of decision making.

2. Discuss specifically the primary director, the primary motivator and the primary regulator of a "pure" market economy.

3. Explain how one type of economic system may include characteristics of the other systems.

4. Evaluate the advantages and disadvantages of each of the three basic economic systems.

5. Describe the four factors of production. What is the payment for the use of each factor called?

6. What are some of the causes of the continuing imbalance between human wants and resources.

7. How may greater efficiency in the production of goods (increased amount produced in a given period of time) be achieved?

8. Compare and contrast three usually accepted economic goals.

9. Explain the three basic economic questions that must be answered by all organized societies.

10. Discuss the factors that primarily limit a society's level of economic satisfaction or output.

11. What is meant by opportunity cost? Give an example.

12. Why does interdependence of members of a society usually increase with the improvement in economic well-being of the members of that society?

For reference, use List of Economic Understandings for this Concept Area.

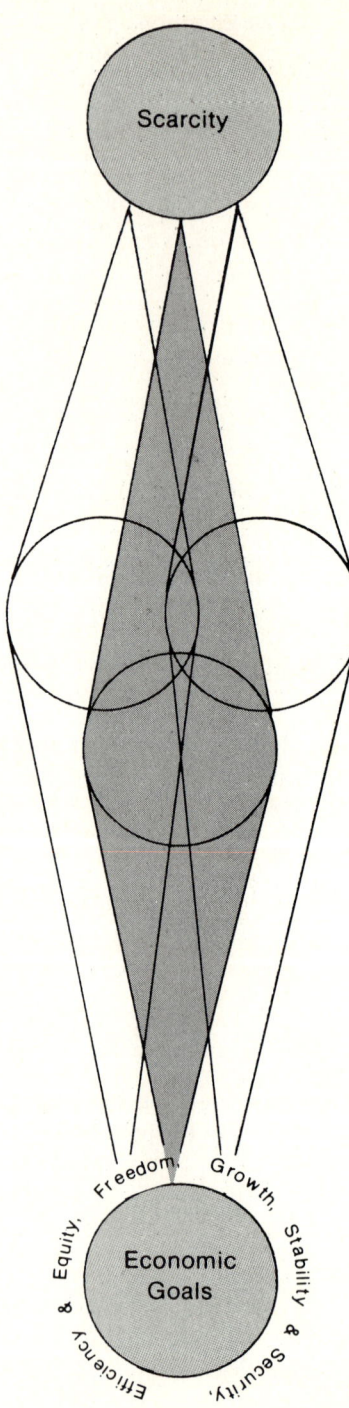

– Producer and Manager of Production (Producer of output and consumer of that output.)

Complete code of screenings for Model on Page 6.

# DEMAND AND SUPPLY: THE MARKET IN OPERATION

## Concept Area II

### Contents

**OVERVIEW OF CONCEPT AREA II**   34

    Market Demand   34
    Price Elasticity   34
    Market Supply   35
    Equilibrium Price   36
    Functions of Price   36
    Competition and Price   37

**LIST OF ECONOMIC UNDERSTANDINGS IN CONCEPT AREA II**   38

**TEACHING APPLICATIONS IN CONCEPT AREA II**   39

    **University Level Instruction**   39

        1. A Demand Derivation Activity   39
        2. A Supply Derivation Activity   41
        3. A Price Determination Activity   43
        4. An Activity on the Functions of Price   44

    **Secondary Level Instruction**   46

        1. An Activity on the Market Structures in the American Economic System   46
        2. Wheat Game (Supply and Demand)   47
        3. Geologist Dilemma   51

    **Elementary Level Instruction**   52

        1. An Auction   52
        2. Trade-offs (Lesson 10-13)   53

**EVALUATION INSTRUMENT OF CONCEPT AREA II**   56

# OVERVIEW OF CONCEPT AREA II

**MARKET DEMAND.** *Demand* is the various amounts of a product or service that an individual is able and willing to purchase at different prices in a given period of time when all other factors that affect demand remain unchanged. Among the factors affecting demand are income, taste, prices of all other goods that could be bought, the availability of the product and other products, the cost of borrowing. Thus, when demand for a specific product is determined, these factors are held constant in order to isolate the relationship between the quantity demanded of the product at the various possible prices for that product. Once these factors or just one of them is allowed to change, the amounts that are demanded at the various prices may also change in response to the change that has occurred. Each of these factors affects the demand for the product (i.e. the relationship between the amounts and prices) in a different manner depending on whether they increase the desire for the product or reduce it.

In most cases the *law of demand* governs the amount of a particular product demanded at the various prices such that, as the price of the product increases a smaller quantity of the product is demanded. In order to arrive at the total market demand for a product, all the individual quantities demanded at each price are added together. Thus, the shape of the final market demand for a product will incorporate the individual demands of all individuals, households, and firms that are part of that market and will be downwardly sloping.

**PRICE ELASTICITY.** The responsiveness of the quantity demanded of a product to a price change of that product is known as the *price elasticity of demand*. If more money would be spent at lower prices than at higher prices, demand is relatively elastic. This is true since $2.00 would be spent at a price of 20 cents while $1.00 would be spent at a price of 50 cents each.

An example will illustrate elasticity:

|  | Price of Soft Drink per Bottle | Total Bottles Bought | Total Amount Spent at each Price |
|---|---|---|---|
| Relatively Elastic Demand | .50 | 2 | $1.00 |
|  | .20 | 10 | $2.00 |
| Relatively Inelastic Demand | .10 | 15 | $1.50 |
|  | .05 | 20 | $1.00 |

## Demand and Supply: The Market in Operation

This example determines price elasticity by the total revenue method. A more precise measurement of the amount of price elasticity can be made by using a price elasticity coefficient. Such coefficient compares the percentage change in quantity with the percentage change in price.

$$\text{Price elasticity coefficient} = \frac{\text{percentage change in quantities}}{\text{percentage change in prices}}$$

If a small percentage change in the price of a product results in a larger percentage change in the quantity demanded, then demand is said to be relatively elastic. If price is cut 4 per cent while quantity demanded rises by 8 per cent, the coefficient is:

$$\frac{8\%}{-4\%} = -2.0$$

Price and quantity vary in opposite directions so the coefficients are negative. Any coefficient greater than –1.0 indicates a relatively elastic demand; a coefficient of less than –1.0 indicates a relatively inelastic demand. Identical percentage changes in quantity demanded and price creates a –1.0 coefficient or unitary elasticity.

A necessary good would tend to have an inelastic demand while a luxury good would tend to have an elastic demand. The main factors that determine demand elasticity or inelasticity are urgency for product, need and the availability of substitutes for the product. We would expect the demand for a prescription drug needed by a sick child to be highly inelastic, while we would expect to find the demand for tickets to an amusement park (for the same child when well) to be very elastic.

**MARKET SUPPLY.** *Supply* is the various amounts of a product or service that a producer is able and willing to offer for sale at different prices in a given period of time when all factors that affect supply remain unchanged. These factors that have to remain unchanged are the technology used to produce the product, the prices of the factors of production used to produce the product, the number of producers that supply the product, the prices of other goods and services, etc. When any of these factors change, they influence the various amounts of the product that would be supplied at different prices. Usually the higher the price of a product, the greater is the quantity supplied of the product. This relationship is called the *Law of Supply*. This is the usual case because a producer is able and willing to offer more of a given product to the market at the higher price. In order to arrive at the total supply of a product, all the individual quantities supplied at each price are added together. The shape of the final supply curve will be upsloping (increased supply with increased price) because producers operate at different levels of efficiency and buy their factors of production at different prices.

**EQUILIBRIUM PRICE.** Product prices are determined by the interaction of supply and demand in the market place. The market place does not refer to a specific geographical location but is rather an abstract concept that covers every location in which the product is bought and sold. The price of a product that will prevail in the market, usually referred to as the *equilibrium price*, is that price which simultaneously allows all suppliers to sell the amount that they are able and willing to sell at that price, and all buyers to purchase the amounts that they are willing and able to purchase at that price. This is said to clear the market. The equilibrium price is the only price that could perform that task because at any higher price the quantity supplied will be higher than the quantity demanded and some suppliers will not be able to sell their product. When the price of the product is above the equilibrium price (quantity demanded is less than quantity supplied at the price), there is a downward or reduced demand pressure on the price and eventually price is bid down to the equilibrium price. Conversely, if the price is lower than the market price, then the quantity demanded would be larger than the quantity supplied. This condition would exert an upward pressure on the price since some of the demand remains unsatisfied, and that demand would bid the price up to the equilibrium price. Therefore, the market is said to clear at the equilibrium price where the quantity demanded of a good or service equals the quantity supplied.

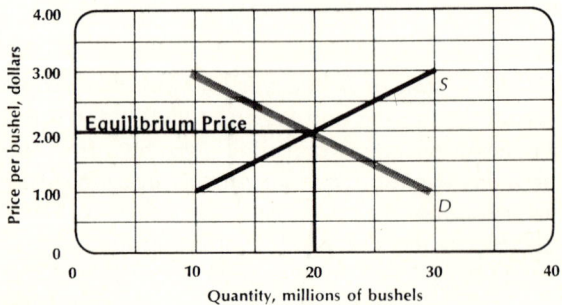

**FUNCTIONS OF PRICE.** Price performs three important functions in the market. The first function is *allocation* of resources. It is apparent that as the value of a given resource is higher in one use than in another, those resources will be pulled to the higher-priced use. The second function of price is that of *rationing*. Individuals who choose to buy a product at a price below the equilibrium price, or who cannot match the equilibrium price, are rationed out of the market. Finally, the third function of price is that of *income distribution.* As the market mechanism determines the value of a product, the value or price of the factors of production necessary to produce the product are also determined. These prices of the factors of production constitute the income to the household units who own the resources. Income will be discussed in the next chapter.

**COMPETITION AND PRICE.** A high level of *competition* among producers of a product will permit the supply and demand conditions in the market to set the prices. The more competition there is between suppliers with knowledge of each others' actions and the more indifferent consumers are to brand names and artificial differentiation between products, the lower will be the equilibrium market price. The presence of profits in pure competition draws new firms into production. This will increase industry supply, and, other things being equal, lower price. In the American economy, we see this criterion materialize especially in agricultural markets. In some of the other markets, the monopoly power of large government units, large business and large unions may result in higher prices and higher wages than the free market would determine. It is hard to generalize about the degree of competition in the American economy as each market has its own special characteristics that are unique to it.

## LIST OF ECONOMIC UNDERSTANDINGS IN CONCEPT AREA II

1. Demand is based on the consumer's ability and willingness to purchase a product. Demand can be thought of as the quantities of a product that will be bought at various prices at any one time.

2. Total or aggregate market demand is the summation of all individual demands.

3. A change in the price of the product will result in a change in the quantity of that product consumers are willing and able to buy. If the price increases the quantity demanded declines and vice versa.

4. A change in income, taste, prices of other goods, etc. results in a change in demand, i.e., a change in the whole list of price/quantity combinations.

5. Supply is a schedule of amounts sellers will offer to sell at each of various possible prices at any one time, other factors remaining unchanged. As with demand, there are changes in quantity supplied as price alone changes. Changes in costs of the factors of production, natural disasters, changes in technology, etc., result in a change in supply — or in the whole list of price/quantity combinations.

6. The equilibrium price of a product is determined by the interaction of supply and demand in the market place. That is, the demand schedule and supply schedule are viewed together. The equilibrium price is the only price that will clear the market; that is, all those who wish to sell and all those who wish to buy at a given price are satisfied.

7. Price elasticity of demand measures responsiveness of the quantity demanded to changes in price.

8. The three important functions of price are:
    a. allocations of resources.
    b. rationing of resources.
    c. income distribution.

9. The American economy consists of markets with differing degrees of competition. This varying competition affects the demand and the supply and, therefore, the particular market equilibrium price.

# TEACHING APPLICATIONS IN CONCEPT AREA II

## University Level Instruction

### A Demand Derivation Activity

The student will be able to understand that:

> *Primary Economic Understanding:* Demand for a particular product is a listing of the quantities of that product that a consumer is willing and able to purchase at the various possible prices for that product over a given period of time when everything else is held constant.

> *Secondary Economic Understanding:* Consumers' wants are considered demand only if they have the ability and willingness to purchase the product that satisfies these events.
>
> At lower prices consumers usually purchase a larger amount of the product.
>
> Factors other than price may affect the demand for the product; when these factors change, the entire demand will also change for each price.
>
> The total demand for a product reflects the quantity demanded by all consumers at particular prices.

*Purpose:* This learning activity is constructed to guide the student through an exercise that will demonstrate that demand reflects the willingness and ability (preferences) of consumers to buy.

*Materials and Instructions:*

1. Allocate a certain amount of money to each of three groups representing three different income levels.
2. Students indicate how many tape cassettes they are willing and able to buy at each price on the chart.
3. After completing the table find the Total Market and construct a

## 40 Demand and Supply: The Market in Operation

demand curve on graph paper. Each price and quantity will represent a point on the curve.

| Price per Cassette | Person 1 | Person 2 | Person 3 | Person 4 | Person 5 | Person 6 | Person 7 | Total Market |
|---|---|---|---|---|---|---|---|---|
| $10,000 | | | | | | | | |
| $ 8,000 | | | | | | | | |
| $ 6,000 | | | | | | | | |
| $ 4,000 | | | | | | | | |
| $ 2,000 | | | | | | | | |
| 0 | | | | | | | | |

4. Using the following demand schedule construct a demand curve.

### Demand Schedule for Tape Cassettes

| Price | Market Demand |
|---|---|
| $10 | 2,000 |
| 9 | 3,500 |
| 8 | 4,000 |
| 7 | 5,700 |
| 6 | 6,200 |
| 5 | 10,000 |
| 4 | 12,000 |
| 3 | 15,000 |

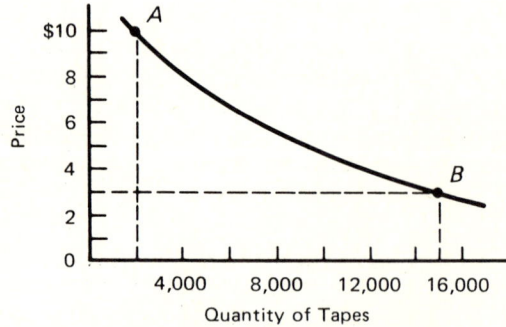

Figure 1 The Demand for Tape Cassettes*

---

*M.H. McCarty, *Dollars and Sense*, Scott, Foresman & Co., 1979. Reprinted by permission.

### Demand and Supply: The Market in Operation

*Economic Content and Debriefing:*

1. Each individual's demand is a reflection of a personal preference for the product with both the willingness and ability to buy. Consumers with different preferences and tastes choose different amounts at the same price. Use this observation to discuss how individual willingness to buy, as well as ability to buy influence demand.

2. The law of demand is illustrated by the demand curve, namely, at higher prices, the quantity demand decreases and at lower prices the quantity demanded increases.

3. The teacher may increase the incomes of the individual and make a new demand schedule. The entire list of quantities demanded at each price will increase. This is an *increase in demand*.

 Ask the class to list other factors than can influence their demand other than income. This list might include the price of records (a substitute good), the price of cassette players (a complementary good), expectations of changes in price of cassette players or new technologies, changes in life style, or changes in the number of students in the class (population). If there is an increase in demand, the entire demand curve will shift to the right. If there is a decrease in demand the entire curve will shift to the left.

4. The total demand for cassettes is the sum of each row. This shows how market demand reflects the demand of each individual for cassettes.

**A Supply Derivation Activity**

The student will be able to understand that:

> *Primary Economic Understanding:* At higher prices suppliers will be willing and able to offer a larger quantity of the product on the market.
>
> *Secondary Economic Understanding:* Supply is a list of quantities that producers are willing and able to offer on the market at the various possible prices over a given period of time, everything else held constant.

*Purpose:* This activity is constructed to show the student that producers will offer a larger quantity of a particular product at higher prices, because costs of producing each additional item increase.

*Materials and Instructions:*

1. Using the supply schedule construct a supply curve.
2. Ask students to list ways to increase production as the result of a large sale reported by the Sales Department.

## 42 Demand and Supply: The Market in Operation

3. Prepare a new supply schedule for increasing the supply of cassettes produced and construct a new supply curve on the same graph.

**Supply Schedule for Tape Cassettes**

| Price | Market Demand |
|-------|---------------|
| $10   | 17,500        |
| 9     | 16,000        |
| 8     | 15,000        |
| 7     | 13,000        |
| 6     | 11,000        |
| 5     | 10,000        |
| 4     | 7,000         |
| 3     | 5,000         |

**Market Supply**

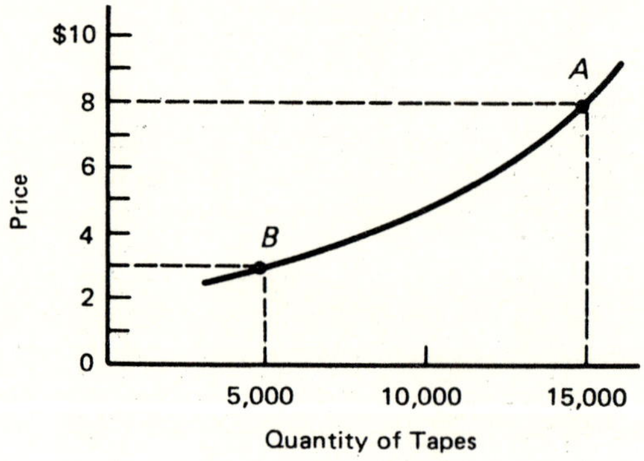

Figure 2 The Supply of Tape Cassettes*

4. Interpret the graphs in terms of the economic content.

*Economic Content and Debriefing:*

1. Additional resources for increasing production will cost more than the previous units. For example, when workers are paid the overtime rate the cost will be 150% of the regular wage rate.

2. As a result, profits will be lower unless the price is increased sufficiently to cover the additional costs including a profit, otherwise the manager will not be willing and able to supply the additional units.

---

*M.H. McCarty, *Dollars and Sense*, Scott, Foresman & Co., 1979. Reprinted by permission.

3. Given a limited capacity for production, the law of supply states that the supplier will be willing and able to supply a larger quantity only if the price of the product increases.

4. Profit is the prime determinant of the willingness and ability to supply.

**A Price Determination Activity:**

The student will understand that:

> *Primary Economic Understanding:* The price of a product is determined in the market through the interaction of supply and demand.
>
> *Secondary Economic Understanding:* The market price, equilibrium price, is the only price at which the quantity supplied will be equal to the quantity demanded.
>
> Any interference with the market price, such as a price ceiling or price floor will result in a shortage or surplus, respectively, in the market.

*Purpose:* This graph is constructed to illustrate the price determination situation.

*Materials and Instructions:*

1. Using the demand curve, Fig. 1, and the supply curve, Fig. 2, in the two previous activities prepare a graph to illustrate the equilibrium price.

2. Assume that a price control (price ceiling) is set by the government at $4.00. Describe the economic behavior that follows, explaining how and why the price is restored to equilibrium.

3. Assume that a price floor is set by the government at $7.00. Analyze the economic behavior that follows, explaining how and why the price is restored to equilibrium.

**Market Demand**

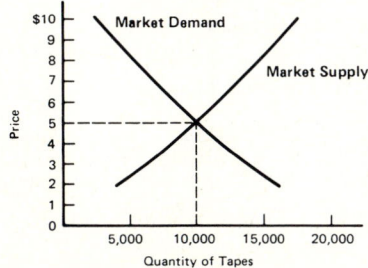

**Figure 3  Market Equilibrium***

---

*M.H. McCarty, *Dollars and Sense*, Scott, Foresman & Co., 1979. Reprinted by permission.

## 44 Demand and Supply: The Market in Operation

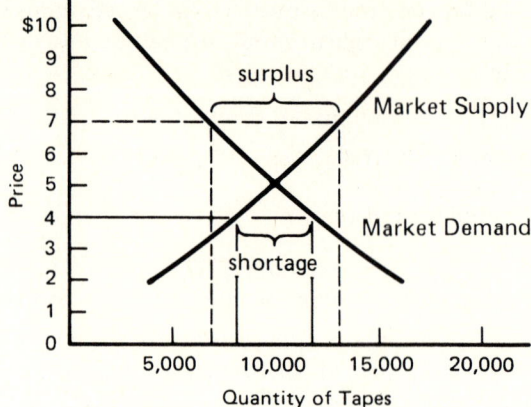

Figure 4 Surpluses and Shortages*

*Economic Content and Debriefing:*

1. The students will look at prices, other than the equilibrium and discover that if the price is set at a point higher than equilibrium, the quantity supplied will be greater than the quantity demanded at that price and there will be a surplus. Because of large inventories, prices of the cassettes will be reduced to clear the surplus until the price declines to equilibrium. At the lower price more persons are willing and able to buy the cassettes. If the price is set at a point that is lower than equilibrium price, the quantity supplied will be less than the quantity demanded and there will be a shortage. Persons who are willing to pay a higher price will bid up the price to equilibrium. The market forces distribute the cassettes to those who are willing and able to pay the higher price.

2. Use these graphs to illustrate the various effects on price when market conditions change, such as changes in income, a new technology, an innovation, etc., and where there is a change in quantity demanded.

**An Activity on the Functions of Price**

The student will be able to understand that:

> *Primary Economic Understanding:* The market system answers most of the economic decisions it faces through the use of prices.
>
> *Secondary Economic Understanding:* The scarce resources in a market system are allocated to their best possible use through the use of prices.

---

*M.H. McCarty, *Dollars and Sense*, Scott, Foresman & Co., 1979. Reprinted by permission.

## Demand and Supply: The Market in Operation

In a market system goods and services are consumed by those who can afford to pay their prices. Factors of production earn a price on the market just like any other product. These are called costs.

*Purpose:* This activity was constructed to show the student that the three functions of a price are:
   1. allocator of resources
   2. rationer of resources
   3. distributor of income

*Materials and Instructions:*

1. Have the students select a particular product for example a particular automobile which has a market price of $6,000.
2. Pose the following questions to the class:
    a. What materials are used in the production of the automobile?
    b. Why were these materials used in production of that car instead of any other product?
    c. Can a consumer purchase that product if the maximum price the customer was willing to pay for it was $5,400?
    d. Does the price of the car influence the pay of workers who manufactured it? Does the wage of the auto worker affect the price of the automobile?
3. Each student should answer each question, and then the topic could be opened for discussion by the whole class.

*Economic Content and Debriefing:*

1. Questions 2.a and 2.b address themselves to the function of price as an allocator of resources. The questions show the complexity of the allocation problem as the auto-producer has to bid away all these resources from their alternative uses. For example, the auto-producer has to attract the steel from the producer of knife blades, the plastic from the toy manufacturer, etc. This is a subtle function of the price of the car as, had it been lower, then the car manufacturers would not have been able to attract all these resources. This is a guarantee that resources will be utilized for their best use because other producers would be able to pay a higher price for them if they could use them in a more profitable way. This explains the efficiency of prices in allocating resources between their various alternative uses.

2. Questions 2.c and 2.d address the same price function in the consumer products market. Everyone would like to own a new car. The problem is

## 46   Demand and Supply: The Market in Operation

who will, since there aren't enough cars to satisfy everyone's wishes. The price of the car performs this rationing function by allowing individuals to evaluate their needs for this car, and determine the amount of other products they are willing to forgo in order to own this car. Those who are willing to forgo other products valued at no less than $6,000 will be able to purchase the product. Those who are not willing to do without the other products will be rationed out of the market. This explains how resources are rationed between the many consumers through the use of prices. The price of the automobile determines the wage of the workers.

## Secondary Level Instruction

**An Activity on the Market Structures in the American Economic System:**

The student should be able to understand that:

> *Primary Economic Understanding:* The various market structures can be arranged in a continuum from structures with characteristics of pure competition to structures that have strong characteristics of a monopoly.
>
> *Secondary Economic Understanding:* In reality there is no pure competition and no pure monopoly in any economic system. All structures are a mixture of competition and monopoly ranging from a high degree of competition to a high degree of monopoly.

*Purpose:* To enable students to understand the variations in competitive and pricing characteristics which explain their behavior in the market.

*Materials and Instructions:*
1. Categorize a list of businesses according to the market power that each has and arrange the groups on the chart from the least on the left to the most on the right. Grouping of firms may be oriented to the following:
   a. The number of firms in the industry
   b. The ease of entry
   c. The knowledge of the market
   d. The amount of control over price
   e. The differentiation of the product
2. Arrange the groups in a continuum from the least market power for the individual to the greatest market power.

## Demand and Supply: The Market in Operation

3. Point out the characteristics of competition and monopoly for each group.

| Pure Competition | Imperfect Competition | | Pure Monopoly |
|---|---|---|---|
| + | ease of entry | — | |
| + | no. of firms | — | |
| — | knowledge of market | + | |
| — | control over price | + | |
| — | differentiation of product | + | |

*Economic Content and Debriefing:*

1. Analysis gives the student an opportunity to generalize about the characteristics of firms in the market in an orderly manner for the purpose of understanding their behavioral patterns.

2. Analysis will include a comparison of production levels, pricing techniques, and competition.

3. Distinguish between market structures—pure competition, imperfect competition, and pure monopoly—according to the characteristics in Item 1, Materials and Instruction.

4. Recognize from the analysis that pure competition and pure monopoly do not exist. Each of the market structures has a combination of competition and monopoly in different amounts.

**Wheat Game***

The student will be able to understand that:

*Primary Economic Understanding:* Market Price is determined in a free market by the interaction of supply and demand.

*Secondary Economic Understanding:* The value of a product varies considerably among consumers. Likewise the ability to produce varies considerably among suppliers.

---

*Wheat Game:* Joint Council on Economic Education. This exercise is available in *Teachers Manual, Readings in Economics for 12th Grade Students of American Democracy* (Pittsburgh DEEP materials), and in *American Economic Review* (May, 1965).

## 48    Demand and Supply: The Market in Operation

*Purpose:* The object of the game is to introduce students to the mechanics of the market mechanism in a more inviting way than through lectures or readings. Specifically it illustrates that in a perfectly competitive market the forces of supply and demand push the price of wheat to a point of equilibrium, that point or price where the quantity demanded by buyers is equal to the quantity which sellers are willing and able to supply.

*Materials and Instructions:*

The following materials are needed:

1. Instructions: The instructions which appear below should be duplicated, in sufficient quantity, so that each participant in the game will have a copy.
2. Record Form: The Record Form, which appears on page 50, is needed to keep a permanent record of the transactions made.
3. Buyer Identification Tags: Lapel tags labeled "Buyer" need to be made for all buyers in the game; the game summarized here will accommodate up to thirty-six buyers.
4. Containers for Buy Orders and Sell Orders: Two containers (paper bags) one labeled "Buy Orders" and the other labeled "Sell Orders" are needed. The instructor should point out why buyers and sellers would come to the market with different buying or selling price intentions.
5. Buy Orders: These orders can be conveniently placed on 3 x 5 file cards. On one side of all the cards write "Buy Order", the order is placed on the opposite side of all the cards according to the following schedule:

4 cards at each price

"Buy 1,000 bushels of wheat for *not more than* $1.20 per bushel."
"     "      "      "     "       "      "       "    $1.40  "      "
"     "      "      "     "       "      "       "    $1.60  "      "
"     "      "      "     "       "      "       "    $1.80  "      "
"     "      "      "     "       "      "       "    $2.00  "      "
"     "      "      "     "       "      "       "    $2.20  "      "
"     "      "      "     "       "      "       "    $2.40  "      "
"     "      "      "     "       "      "       "    $2.60  "      "
"     "      "      "     "       "      "       "    $2.80  "      "

Total Number of "Buy Orders" = 36

## Demand and Supply: The Market in Operation 49

6. Sell Orders: These orders can be conveniently placed on 3 x 5 cards. On one side of all the cards write "Sell Orders", the order is placed on the opposite side of the card according to the following schedules:

4 cards at each price
"Sell 1,000 bushels of wheat for not less than $1.20 per bushel."
    "      "      "      "    $1.40  "  "
    "      "      "      "    $1.60  "  "
    "      "      "      "    $1.80  "  "
    "      "      "      "    $2.00  "  "
    "      "      "      "    $2.20  "  "
    "      "      "      "    $2.40  "  "
    "      "      "      "    $2.60  "  "
    "      "      "      "    $2.80  "  "

Total Number of "Sell Orders" = 36

*Procedures in Playing the Game*

Before the game is started three tasks need to be accomplished. First, the teacher needs to determine how many trading sessions to conduct and the length of each trading session. If one is willing to allocate two class periods to playing the game it seems reasonable that four, fifteen-minute trading sessions can be executed. The number and length of the trading sessions, of course, can be altered to suit different circumstances. Second, the teacher needs to assign the various roles in the game. One student is needed to record the transactions on the chalkboard; the remaining students are put into the two groups, buyers and sellers. The teacher is free to oversee the operation of the game, and answer students' questions. Once the student roles are assigned the "Instructions" can be given to the students to read. The game can now be played.

## STUDENT INSTRUCTIONS

You are about to participate in the operation of a commodity market. You will be given an order to buy or sell 1,000 bushels of wheat under certain conditions. In general, you should not reveal your instructions to any of the other dealers, unless you have particular reason for doing so. You should consider yourself to be an agent, acting in behalf of a client who has given you specific instructions. You have an obligation to do as well as you can for your client, and you are not permitted to violate instructions.

When the market opens, at the signal of the instructor, you may proceed to carry out your order. Buyers will be identified by a lapel tag. A transaction is completed when a single buyer and a single seller agree on

## RECORD FORM

Trading Session (circle one):  1  2  3  4

| Transaction Number | Price |
|---|---|
| 1 | _____ |
| 2 | _____ |
| 3 | _____ |
| 4 | _____ |
| 5 | _____ |
| 6 | _____ |
| TOTAL | _____ |
| AVERAGE | _____ |

the terms of the sale. As soon as you report and record a transaction, report to the recorder so that you may report and record your transaction. As soon as your transaction is reported, you should turn in your buy or sell order and receive a new one of the same kind. You may proceed immediately to complete a new transaction in accordance with your new order. If you are unable to complete a transaction within 5 minutes, you may obtain a new order from your instructor.

When the market is closed, the instructor will determine and report whether the buyers or sellers have represented their clients more successfully.

Prices must be rounded off to the nearest 10¢.

*Economic Content and Debriefing*

1. The central point of the game is to see what happens to the average price per bushel of wheat determined in each session in relation to the equilibrium prices ($2.00). The average price is calculated by summing all the transaction prices for one trading session and dividing the sum by the number of transactions.

If the average price is above the equilibrium price the sellers are making an unusually large profit at the expense of the buyer; if, on the other hand, the average price is below the equilibrium then the buyers are profiting at the expense of the sellers. While the students should not during the game be told what the equilibrium price is, they should be informed of the average price for each session. Over the trading sessions that average should tend toward, if not arrive at, the point of equilibrium where at $2.00 per bushel 20,000 bushels are demanded and supplied.

## Geologist Dilemma*

The student will understand that:

*Primary Economic Understanding:* The supply of resources exist in various amounts and in all cases supply is limited.

*Secondary Economic Understanding:* The amount of any resource offered to the market depends on price. There may be social costs associated with natural resource depletion.

*Purpose:* This activity will demonstrate how the supply of various energy sources is limited and how the rising cost to secure increasing amounts of energy in combination with an increase in demand for energy causes the price of various energy supplies to rise.

*Materials and Instructions:*

Beads and corn meal are placed in a container in the following proportions:

| | | |
|---|---|---|
| Black beads (coal) | 50% | Company I |
| Red beads (uranium) | 3% | Company II |
| White beads (natural gas) | 10% | Company III |
| Blue beads (oil) | 37% | Company IV |
| Corn meal (solar) | 1 TBSP. | Company V |

The beads and corn meal are thrown into the air. Divide the class into 5 companies — each of which will search for one color bead. (Do not interfere if some collect far more than another company.) These beads and corn meal represent an unknown quantity of energy reserves.

Instruct the companies to search for resources for one minute. Sort resources into separate piles. Count resource and record the totals for each group.

Second round — search for one minute.

Third round and final round — search for one minute each.

Some of the energy resources will be easier to collect than others. The collection of additional resources in Rounds 2, 3, and 4 become progressively difficult because of scarcity. Costs increase and efforts are made to increase the productivity, i.e., accumulating more resources in the same time period. The result is a rise in price. There is a depletion of resources and disruption of the environment. The social costs are compared with the value of the resource for arriving at a decision to continue to accumulate the resources.

---

*The Geoligist's Dilemma *Energy Tradeoffs in the Marketplace.* Wentworth, Leonard & Deming, 1980, p. 5-1.

## 52  Demand Supply: The Market in Operation

*Economic Content and Debriefing:*

1. Energy supplies are limited and exist in varying amounts.

2. As energy becomes more scarce and demand for energy continues to increase price will rise.

3. More energy may be secured with the addition of technology and capital goods to the collection process.

4. The cost of accumulation of resources reflect scarcity and the difficulty of collecting them.

5. There is a depletion of resources and disruption of the environment when energy supplies are secured.

6. The associated social costs to the procurement of energy can be compared to the value of the resource supply.

## Elementary Level Instruction

**An Auction**

The student will be able to understand that:

> *Primary Economic Understanding:* The price of a product is determined through the interaction of supply and demand in the marketplace.
> *Secondary Economic Understanding:* Demand is based on the consumer's willingness and ability to buy a product; this willingness is influenced by one's tastes and preferences.
> *Secondary Economic Understanding:* The law of demand implies that at higher prices consumers tend to buy less.

*Purpose:* This activity is designed to show the elementary student that prices are determined by both supply and demand. In this case, the supply will be fixed at one item. This should be an item of high interest to the students.

*Materials and Instructions:*

1. Have an item available which is likely to generate interest and curiosity from your students. Ask "How many would want to have this item? How could you 'pay' for it?"

2. Students might decide to pay for the item with units of time which would be used to perform classroom jobs. One unit, for example, might equal ten minutes of work.

Demand Supply: The Market in Operation    53

3.    **Demand For Item**

| Units of work (or price) | # of students who would pay ea. price (Qty. demanded) |
|---|---|
| 100 | 1 |
| 90 | 1 |
| 70 | 3 |
| 50 | 5 |
| 25 | 10 |
| 10 | 20 |
| 5 | 25 |
| 3 | 28 |
| 1 | 30 |

Ask students "Who would be willing to pay 100 units of work for this item? 50 units?" and so on. Derive a schedule similar to the one shown above.

4. Ask "What do you notice about the pattern we see here?" Students should be able to articulate the idea that at the higher prices people weren't willing to purchase the item. At the lower prices, more people were both willing and able to buy.

5. "What would cause you to be willing to pay more for an item?" Students should see that their desire for/preference for certain items influences their willingness to pay more. Advertising and popular "in" items influence tastes.

6. "If an item is scarce (such as the one being used today) and many people want it and are willing and able to pay for it, what is likely to happen to the price of the item?" The price will be bid higher by those consumers competing against one another for the available item.

**Trade-offs (Lessons 10-13)***

The student will understand that:

*Primary Economic Understanding:* Market prices influence decisions pertaining to what goods and services will be produced, how they will be produced, and how they will be distributed.

*Secondary Economic Understanding:* The market clearing price for a product is established through the interaction of supply and demand.

---

*\*Trade-offs* consists of a series of fifteen 20-minute television/film programs produced by the Agency for Instructional Television, Bloomington, Indiana.

## 54  Demand Supply: The Market in Operation

*Purpose:* These four film lessons are designed to help students understand market prices—factors that influence prices and how prices, in turn, influence decisions pertaining to how scarce resources are used.

*Materials and Instructions:* The four films "To Buy or Not to Buy," "To Sell or Not to Sell," "At What Price," and "How Could That Happen," comprise Lessons 10-13 of the *Trade-offs* television/film program for 9 to 13 year-olds. For information pertaining to the schedule for airing on local television, contact the State Department of Public Instruction. The films along with a Teacher's Guide are also available for purchase from the producer, the Agency for Instructional Television.

In the film "To Buy or Not to Buy" (Lesson 10), a situation involving a group of students attempting to raise money for a class trip is used as the vehicle for introducing the concept market demand. It also illustrates the effects of such factors as tastes, income, advertising, and the price of other products on market demand. Market supply is introduced and dealt with in a similar manner in the film "To Sell or Not to Sell" (Lesson 11). In both films special visuals are used to acquaint students with graphic representations of consumer and producer behavior in the marketplace.

Again through dramatization of activities of enterprising youngsters and through special visuals, the film "At What Price" (Lesson 12) illustrates how supply and demand interact to establish a market clearing price.

The film "How Could That Happen" (Lesson 13) reinforces concepts dealt with in the three previous films. The interdependence of market prices is emphasized and presented in a manner so as to enable students to see how the "invisible hand" of market forces influences their lives.

*Economic Content and Debriefing:*

1. Market demand refers to the amounts of a product or service people are willing to buy at various prices at any one time. If price is the only factor that changes, consumers will buy more at lower prices and vice versa. If other factors change (e.g., income, tastes, etc.) the market demand will also change.

2. Market supply refers to the amounts of a product or service people are willing to sell at various prices at any one time. If the price is the only factor that changes, producers will sell more at higher prices and vice versa. If other factors change (e.g., the cost of materials, the cost of labor, etc.) the market supply will change according to how the change affects profits.

3. Market clearing price (the equilibrium price) refers to the price at which the amount of a good people are willing to sell is equal to the amount that people are willing to buy. It is the price at which there is neither a surplus nor a shortage.

4. The market for a certain good or service does not operate in isolation. Changes in supply, demand, and market clearing prices in one market will have an effect on other markets.

56   Demand and Supply: The Market in Operation

## EVALUATION OF CONCEPT AREA II

1. Why are demand and want not the same thing? Describe four factors that determine a product demand.

2. Explain two primary determinants of consumer demand for a particular product. State the Law of Demand.

3. What is meant by a shift in demand? How does that shift in demand affect the price and the quantity of the product sold?

4. What is meant by Supply? State the Law of Supply.

5. What determines equilibrium price of a product sold in a purely competitive market?

6. Discuss the three functions of price.

7. Explain what happens to the quantity demanded and the quantity supplied when the price is set below the equilibrium price.

8. What do we mean when we say there is a shortage of low-cost housing? Is there a shortage of high-cost housing?

9. Explain what happens to price and to quantity sold if there is an increase in demand. Why might demand change?

10. Explain how the market rations a commodity like automobiles?

11. What is meant by an elastic demand?

12. By and large are luxuries apt to enjoy elastic or inelastic demands? Has this anything to do with their price?

13. If the price of pipe tobacco rises, what is apt to be the effect on the demand for pipes. On the demand for cigars?

14. Explain the impact on the price and quantity of a product sold when the level of competition among producers of the product is low?

For reference, use List of Economic Understandings for this Concept Area.

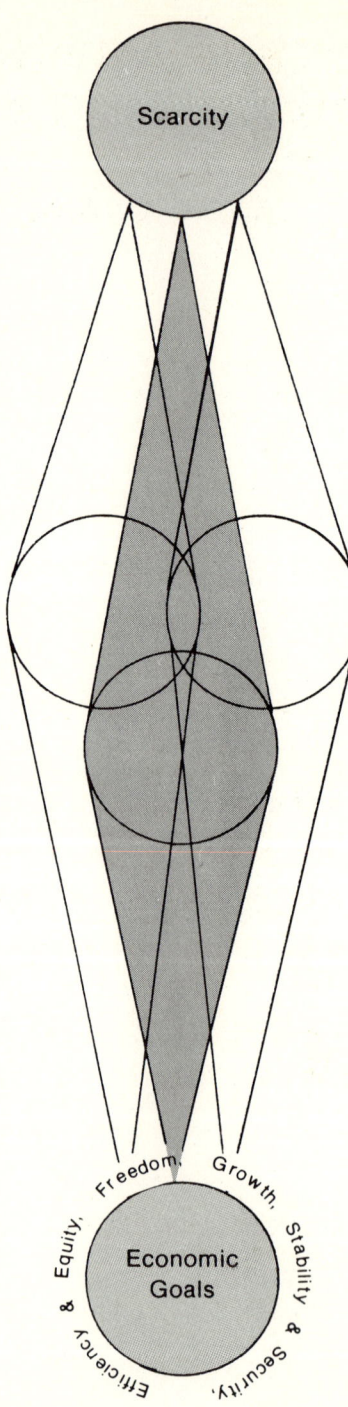

● -Producer and Manager of Production (Producer of output and consumer of that output.)

Complete code of screenings for Model on Page 6.

# INCOME: ORIGINS AND DISTRIBUTIONS

## Concept Area III

## Contents

**OVERVIEW OF CONCEPT AREA III**     60

   Money and Real Income    60
   Price Indexes    60
   National Income Sources    61
   Income Distribution    61
   Income Redistribution    62

**LIST OF ECONOMIC UNDERSTANDINGS IN CONCEPT AREA III**     64

**TEACHING APPLICATIONS IN CONCEPT AREA III**     65

   **University Level Instruction**    65

      1. Settle or Strike    65
      2. Starpower    66
      3. Real Income vs. Money Income    67

   **Secondary Level Instruction**    68

      1. The Protest Movements    68
      2. Newspaper Clipping    71

   **Elementary Level Instruction**    72

      1. Choosing Your Job    72

**EVALUATION INSTRUMENT OF CONCEPT AREA III**     74

# OVERVIEW OF CONCEPT AREA III

**MONEY AND REAL INCOME.** An individual's standard of living is determined by the amount of goods and services that he or she controls. The more goods and services individuals have at their disposal the higher will be their standard of living. The amount of goods and services that an individual commands is referred to as *real income*. Thus, an increase in real income reflects an increase in the total amount of goods and services that an individual commands, taking into account any changes in prices that might have occurred. *Money income* differs from real income in that it does not take into account price changes. Rather, it expresses the goods and services that income commands in dollar values at current market prices. Whereas, when an individual's real income increases we can tell directly that the person's standard of living has improved, however when money income increases it is impossible to determine whether the standard of living has improved, remained the same or declined unless information is made available about the behavior of prices during the time period over which money income increased.

**PRICE INDEXES.** An indicator of changes in the prices of goods and services bought by urban wage earners is compiled monthy by the Bureau of Labor Statistics of the U.S. Department of Labor. This is a weighted average of the prices of hundreds of items called a *Consumer Price Index*. The base period index is 100. Therefore if tne base year is 1967 and the index in a later period is 120, then consumer prices in the later period will be 20% higher on the average than they were in 1967. A person's money income could be translated into real income using the following relationship:

$$\text{Real Income} = \frac{\text{Money Income}}{\text{Price Index}} \times 100$$

An analogous argument applies to the economy as a whole, where the individuals within the economy collectively produce the goods and services to which they have access, thus determining their real income. The key for a nation to achieve a higher standard of living, i.e., a higher real income, is to produce a larger output of goods and services. An economy's money income, like the individual's, does not take into account changes in the prices of goods and services produced.

**NATIONAL INCOME SOURCES.** A country's total income is referred to as *national income* and is classified into payments to the four factors of production—*rent to land; wages to labor; interest to capital;* and *profits to owners or entrepreneurs of business.* The price of each factor of production is basically determined by supply and demand in the market place. The price of the factor of production is considered a cost to the producer and an income to the owner of the factor. Therefore, rent, wages, interest and profits are prices while at the same time income and costs to different sectors of the economy. The sum of payments to the factors of production is the income approach for calculating the Gross National Product.

All persons own at least one factor of production, i.e., their own labor; and most individuals own more than just one. An individual's share of national income depends on the value of the factors of production that the individual controls and sells on the market. Thus the income of one family will depend to some extent on its ability to accumulate private property (capital and natural resources) as well as its own personal labor and entrepreneurial ability. Total family income is determined by the quantity of factor service it has to sell and the price it receives for it in the market.

Each factor of production earns its income by offering its services on that particular factor's market. Thus, a worker earns a wage by offering services to an employer in the labor market. Capital earns interest by allowing a borrower access to its purchasing power. Natural resources earn rent by either providing their mineral rights on the market, or by just allowing someone else access to the space. Finally, entrepreneurial ability earns profits by taking risks in combining the other factors of production to produce goods and services.

The share of each factor of production of national income depends on the proportion that each factor claims of the total cost of producing the goods and services that constitute national income. In 1976, wages accounted for approximately 76.3 percent of national income in the United States. The smallest share was distributed to rental income, which accounts for only 1.7 percent of national income. Interest payments were 6.1 percent, and corporated profits are 8.7 percent of national income. The balance of national income is distributed to both farmers and professionals as proprietors' income which amounts to 7.2 percent of national income.

**INCOME DISTRIBUTION.** One useful method of looking at income distribution is to divide the country into five parts or layers. The highest income of any family that makes up the bottom layer or 20 percent of the nation was $6500 in 1974. This level is called *"near-poverty"* by the Bureau of Labor Statistics. The bottom 20 percent income group is characterized by old age (1/3 of the group consists of retirees), limited education (almost ½ of this group have only grade school education), and a disproportionately large number of the black population and families headed by females or persons under 25 years of age. The next two groups, which make up 40 percent of the population, may be called the *working class*. The income of this 40 percent of the total population was between $6500 and $15,000 in 1974. The two remaining parts above three-fifths of the nation are called *middle class and rich*. If you classify the middle class as families earning between $15,000 and $32,000 a year, the class consists of 35 percent of the population and leaves five percent only for the group called rich (or upper class). This upper class of five percent of the American families had income in 1974 in excess of $32,000 a year.

**INCOME REDISTRIBUTION.** It is the goal of most organized groups within the nation, such as organized labor, manufacturer associations, government agencies, senior citizen groups, welfare recipient groups, etc., to increase their share of national income. It can be seen by an example how some of these groups, *by curtailing competition* and by *using political pressure,* can influence the existing distribution of income and increase their share of national income. A strong barbers' association of owners or employers can prevent an increased supply of barbers from competing effectively with existing barbers, by licensing regulations. The price of haircuts can be kept artificially high, and therefore the barbers' income kept high. Removal of licensing regulations providing for more effective competition by barbers would lower the prices of haircuts and thus reduce barbers' incomes. Control over effective competition in the hands of the barbers' association gives the barbers, instead of impersonal market forces, a significant degree of control over the price of what they have to sell, and, therefore, over their income. This analysis assumes the usual character of demand where consumers prefer more of a good the lower the price.

The government is able to alter the distribution of income among individuals and groups. This task is accomplished by establishing fiscal mechanisms that transfer income among groups and individuals. One example of such a mechanism is the progressive income tax which increases the tax rate a family has to pay on income as income increases. This allows the government to establish welfare programs that aid poor families by transferring some of the government revenues to them, and by making government services available to all individuals regardless of whether they pay taxes or not.

Other redistribution of income techniques include *intervening on the demand side of the market and promotion of programs to improve the productivity of the least skilled and trained.* The most widespread intervention on demand is for labor through the minimum wage. In the last decade, the government has also attempted to alter demand for workers by antidiscrimination, affirmative action laws, and subsidizing on-the-job-training.

The major approach to improving productivity of the least skilled workers is through providing these workers with education, or a specialized training. Where all these approaches to income redistribution have had important impacts, by far the most substantial difference to a large group of the population is from various governmental transfers.

The economic goal of equity is a concern of the entire society; agreement on what exactly is fair or equitable, however, is difficult to reach.

## LIST OF ECONOMIC UNDERSTANDINGS IN CONCEPT AREA III

1. Real income refers to one's actual purchasing power. Money income differs from real income in that it does not reflect price changes.

2. A price index reflects changes in prices of a particular group of goods and services; often such a group is used to indicate an average change in the general price level.

3. National income, as well as Gross National Product, is the sum of payments to the four factors of production.

4. The price of each factor of production is basically determined by supply and demand in the market place.

5. An individual's share of national income depends on the value of the factors of production that the individual controls and sells.

6. A factor of production's share of national income depends on the proportion that each factor claims of the cost of producing national income.

7. Some organized groups within the nation try to increase their share of national income.

8. The government tries to influence the distribution of income among the various groups in the country.

For reference, use List of Economic Understandings for this Concept Area.

# TEACHING APPLICATIONS IN CONCEPT AREA III

## University Level Instruction

**Settle or Strike***

The student will be able to understand that:

> *Primary Economic Understanding:* Collective bargaining is the means of distributing income between the owners and the workers of a particular company.
>
> *Secondary Economic Understanding:* A factor of production's share of the national income depends on the proportion that each factor claims of the cost of producing national income.
>
> Organized groups within the nation try to increase their share of national income.

*Purpose:* This simulation involves students in a realistic collective bargaining session in order to familiarize them with the various strategies involved in collective bargaining.

*Materials and Instructions:* This is a commercially produced simulation game that can be obtained from the publisher. It consists of union and management personality profiles, bargaining cards and instructions. Each negotiating round is followed by a caucus period to allow formulation of new strategies. The instructor's manual includes a key to interpret the outcome of the negotiations.

*Economic Content and Debriefing:*

1. The collective bargaining process involves very complex negotiations between management and unions that encompass many issues. Wages play a focal role in the negotiations; however, there are other issues that are just as important such as union security, vacations and working conditions.

2. The union negotiating teams feel different pressures from the different levels of the union. While the members might feel that a certain issue is paramount and unnegotiable, the international representative might feel differently and exert pressure in favor of another issue.

---

*\*Settle or Strike: a union-management collective bargaining simulation exercise* by Ray Glazier, Games Central. ABT Associates Inc., 55 Wheeler Street, Cambridge, Mass. 02138, 1974.

## 66    Income: Origins and Distributions

3. A high wage settlement might prove beneficial for a union in the short run, however, it could be a detriment in the long run. For example, it could cause the company to close down or move to a different non-unionized location.

4. Outside conditions exert an influence on the bargaining process. For example, if unemployment is high in the region the settlement will be different from that reached if unemployment were at a low level.

5. Each side in the bargaining process has to present a united front even though there might be some disagreement within the ranks on the strategies to be followed.

**Starpower***

The student will be able to understand that:

*Primary Economic Understanding:* Organized groups within the nation try to increase their share of national income.

*Secondary Economic Understanding:* Individuals play more than one role in society; and may find their separate roles are in conflict with each other.

*Purpose:* This simulation presents the conflict that could arise between the various sectors of the economy, as each sector attempts to improve its own position relative to the other sectors.

*Materials and Instructions:* This is a commercially produced game that can be purchased from the publisher. It consists of chips of different values that determine the income level of an individual within the social structure. The amount of points that each individual collects depends on luck, when the chips were first distributed, and one's ability to bargain and barter to increase holdings. Once the distribution is determined, the participants are classified to belong to one of three groups. The squares are the affluent group, the triangles are the poor group, and the circles are the middle group. Some members of the lower groups are able, through a second round of bonus points and barter, to improve their relative position. The classification of groups continues through the game with the squares dominating the game and setting their own rules. This will be in favor of the affluent group.

---

*\*Starpower* by R. Garry Shirts, Simile II, P.O. Box 910, Del Mar, California 92014, 1969.

Income: Origins and Distributions    67

*Economic Content and Debriefing:*

1. The distribution of income in a particular economy tends to be stable over time unless some drastic measure is used to change it.

2. Once a group is classified as being affluent, they will find it easy to continue to be affluent. The poor on the other hand, have difficulty in breaking out of poverty.

3. The social system determines the movement between the various groups. Upward mobility, in terms of income, is dependent on the social systems. Political systems may affect movements.

**Real Income vs. Money Income**

The student will be able to understand that:

> *Primary Economic Understanding:* Real income refers to one's actual purchasing power. Money income differs from real income in that it does not reflect price changes.
>
> *Secondary Economic Understandings:* A price index reflects changes in prices of a particular group of goods and services.
>
> Organized groups within the nation try to increase their share of national income.

*Purpose:* This activity familiarizes the student with the importance of adjusting money income to real terms. It also shows how certain groups in society are relatively more able to adjust to inflation and thus not experience a decline in their standard of living.

*Materials and Instructions*

1. Collect information in different years on the average annual money income of different occupational groups in the country which are of interest to the class.
2. Collect information on the consumer price index for the same years. This information could be obtained from the *Statistical Abstracts of the U. S.* which is updated annually by the Census Bureau.
3. Construct a table from the collected information that will allow the student to determine the real income by deflating the money income with the proper price index using the following relationship:

$$\text{Real income} = \frac{\text{Money income}}{\text{Price index}} \times 100$$

## 68  Income: Origins and Distributions

This table can look as follows:

| Occupation | Money Income 1967 | Money Income 1975 | Price Index 1967 | Price Index 1975 | Real Income 1967 | Real Income 1975 | %change in money income | % change in real income |
|---|---|---|---|---|---|---|---|---|
| | | | | | | | | |
| | | | | | | | | |
| | | | | | | | | |

4. Have students determine the percentage change in both money income and real income.

*Economic Content and Debriefing:*

1. An increase in money income during inflationary periods does not necessarily mean an increase in a family's standard of living.

2. Certain groups are better able to cope with rising prices and thus maintain their standard of living. Have the class identify those groups from the information collected and determine the reasons for success.

3. Extend this concept to the prices of different goods and services that students buy in order to determine which items have increased in price more than the price index and which have increased at a lower rate.

## Secondary Level Instruction

**The Protest Movements\***

The student will be able to understand that:

*Primary Economic Understanding:* The price (income) of each factor of production is determined directly or indirectly by supply and demand in the market place.

*Secondary Economic Understanding:* Organized groups within the nation try to increase their share of national income.

---

*\*The Protest Movements, Topic 10; Teaching Economics in American History,* by George G. Dawson, Edward C. Prehn, Joint Council of Economic Education, New York, New York, 1973.

## Income: Origins and Distributions

*Purpose:* This study unit is designed to illustrate that an individual's share of national income depends on the value of the factors of production that the individual controls.

*Materials and Instructions:* This commercially prepared unit, part of *Teaching Economics in American History* for Secondary Schools, can be secured from the publisher. It consists of a teacher's manual that discusses wage theories of the 19th Century: "iron law of wages", fund theory, marginal productivity theory and bargaining theory; as well as functional distribution of income, to include the structure and role of trade unions. Discussion questions and activities follow the topical narrative. The Unit contains supplemental materials prepared for the teacher as follows:

1. Wall Chart—Functional Distribution of Income.
2. Activity Master 1—How Do We Measure Contributions to Production?
3. Activity Master 2—"How is Labor's Share of Income Determined?"
4. Activity Master 3—"How Does Productivity Affect Income Shares?"

*Economic Content and Debriefing:*

1. Since all four factors of production help produce the national income, each is entitled to a share of it (called Functional Distribution of Income).

2. Profit levels (entrepreneurial share of income) fluctuates whereas the income share of wages, rent and interest tend to be more stable.

3. The National Income Shares are approximately:

| | | |
|---|---|---|
| Wages | — | 75% |
| Rent | — | 2% |
| Interest | — | 7% |
| Profit | — | 5% (after allowance for depreciation and taxes). |

4. Productivity is based on the interrelationship of all factors of production; therefore, the decrease or increase in any one factor affects total output.

5. It is impossible for one factor of production to increase its share of a given level of national income without reducing the share to another factor of production.

6. Units of various factors of production will be added by management according to the relative marginal productivity or value of the added units to production.

## Miner's Council Votes to Accept A New Coal Pact—Newspaper clipping*

The student will be able to understand:

> *Primary Economic Understanding:* Organized monopoly groups are able to exert significant influence on economic issues relative to their employment.
>
> *Secondary Economic Understanding:* Organized public employees often provide services that cannot be interrupted without important adverse affects on the general population.

*Purpose:* This news clipping illustrates to the student that the contract bargaining process of labor-management has unusual and difficult characteristics in the public sector due to the nature of services rendered.

*Materials and Instructions:* Select four to six students to conduct a group study. Provide each group member with a copy of the news clipping. A chairperson should be selected by the students to lead the group discussion. The students should be given a sheet with the following instructions for study:
1. Review the article to:
   Define the problem.
   Point out the conclusions or goals.
2. Identify the relevant economic principles or concepts.
3. Analyze the alternatives.
4. Choose and support your alternatives.
   Point out why you do or do not agree with conclusions of the article.

Allow between thirty and forty-five minutes for group study (overnight assignment is even better); then ask the group or a spokesperson for the group to report the conclusions of the group to the class and lead a discussion with the entire group.

*Economic Content and Debriefing:*

1. Strong organized groups—particularly monopoly groups, are able to artificially hold up prices and increase their share of the national income.

2. Just as equity itself is difficult to define, so whether income is equitably distributed is also difficult to resolve.

3. Labor employed in basic public services required for the general welfare of the society have both advantages and disadvantages in labor-management negotiations.

---

*\*Miners' Council Votes to Accept a New Coal Pact* New York Times, May 29, 1981. Reprinted by permission.

# The New York Times

NEW YORK, SATURDAY, MAY 30, 1981

## Miners' Council Votes to Accept A New Coal Pact

### Rank and File's Approval Needed for Strike to End

**By BEN A. FRANKLIN**
Special to The New York Times

WASHINGTON, May 29 — Leaders of the United Mine Workers today approved a proposed agreement to end a strike by 160,000 coal miners, quickly accepting the terms negotiated with the mine operators early this morning.

At a news conference this afternoon, Sam M. Church Jr., the union's president, called the agreement "probably the best that will be negotiated this year in any industry." He said that the agreement, running to October 1984, would give U.M.W. members a 38 percent increase in wages and benefits and include most of the provisions whose omission in a previous settlement led to its rejection by the rank and file.

The 36-to-2 vote today by the union's bargaining council, a tally then made unanimous, seemed to give the new tentative settlement a better chance of ratification by the soft-coal miners, who struck 64 days ago. A secret-ballot vote by the membership is scheduled for June 6.

### Lost Provision Is Regained

Attempts to overcome the contract issues that led to the previous contract's rejection began in earnest here last Friday.

In seven days of negotiations with Bobby R. Brown, the chief negotiator for the Bituminous Coal Operators Association, Mr. Church was able to gain reinstatement of a contract provision that he lost in previous bargaining. The provision requires companies that buy coal for resale from nonunion mines to pay a tonnage royalty on the coal to the United Mine Workers' health and retirement fund. The fund is financed by royalties on coal from union mines, and the provision in the March contract was viewed by many miners as a threat to the union's existence.

In addition, the industry negotiators partly retreated on another controversial matter: the protection of the union's jurisdiction over construction and maintenance work performed by the employees of subcontractors engaged by the signatory coal companies.

The union's tight control over subcontracting was ruled a violation of antitrust laws by the Federal courts last year. Many miners opposed the first contract because it gave the union no control over subcontracting, though Mr. Church attempted to explain the court decision to them. The language reached in the new agreement is aimed at gaining acceptance of the miners while remaining within the law.

Mr. Brown, president of the Consolidation Coal Company, the largest employer of U.M.W. workers, also gave up a 45-day probationary period for "new hires." He had won the provision in the first round of negotiations, but it was seen by some miners as a possible means of "union busting."

## Elementary Level Instruction

**Choosing Your Job:**

The student will understand that:

> *Primary Economic Understanding:* An individual or household's standard of living is determined by the amount of goods and services that the individual or household controls.
>
> *Secondary Economic Understanding:* The price of each factor of production (including his labor resource) is determined directly and indirectly by supply and demand in the market place.
>
> An individual's share of national income depends on the value of the factors of production (including his labor resource) that he controls.

*Purpose:* Students are made aware of the differences in income between various occupational groups. The activity introduces the student to the different requirements of different occupations.

> *Materials and Instructions:*

Lower elementary level

1. Each student will ask family members about their jobs. They may want to identify the persons as ABCD and list them in order of education and training, income, skills and productivity.
2. At the next grade level they may categorize school personnel and relate each group to income and skills.

Upper elementary level

1. Continue this study as higher grade levels — 4th and above to study income distribution in the community, nation, and the world.
2. Ask each student to write a paragraph or draw a picture about a job possibility that is attractive.
3. Ask the students to research job opportunities — classified ads in the newspaper, classified section in the telephone book, or observations of people at work.
4. Correlate the above research with goals, values, and decisions for job preferences.
5. Discuss the differences in income for different jobs and explain the differences.
6. Apply to career education.

*Economic Content and Debriefing:*

1. Jobs have different content and offer different amenities. The job market is diversified and offers many opportunities for matching job specifications with individual choices and abilities.

2. The jobs that offer a high pay scale have more stringent requirements for which there is a scarcity of labor resources who meet these requirements.

3. When demand increases for labor resources in specific job classifications, such as accountants, the pay is higher because of the competition for the limited supply. As the market adjusts and supply responds to the increased demand, the relative differences in wages stabilize or diminish.

4. The concept of human capital is introduced. Education and training increase the productivity of the work increase, the value of his human resource and, in turn, the income that is distributed to him.

## EVALUATION OF CONCEPT AREA III

1. Why is it impossible for a nation's real income to increase without real output increasing?

2. Is it correct to say that factor payments (rent, interest, wage and profits) are based ultimately on the supply and demand of the factors? Explain.

3. Interpret a Consumer Price Index of 171.

4. What is meant by national income?

5. Explain how one organized group can increase its share of national income.

6. Upon what is individual family income primarily dependent?

7. Distinguish between money and real income.

8. Give an example of income redistribution by government.

9. Which factor of production claims the largest share of national income? Why?

For reference, use List of Economic Understandings for this Concept Area.

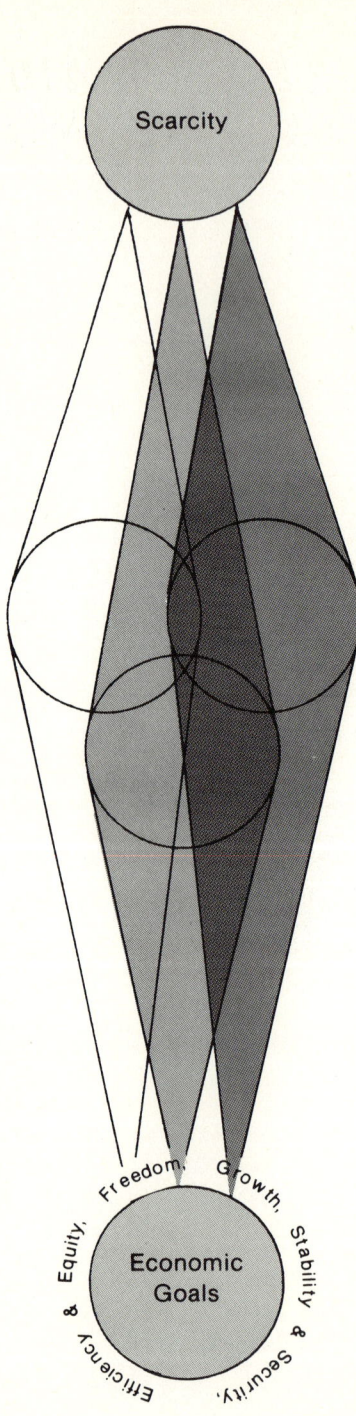

● -Producer and Manager of Production (Producer of output and consumer of that output.)

● -Director of Public Production (Spending and saving programs—as a citizen in one's democratic role.)

Complete code of screenings for Model on Page 6.

# PROFITS, SAVINGS AND ECONOMIC GROWTH

## CONCEPT AREA IV

## Contents

**OVERVIEW OF CONCEPT AREA IV**   78

   **Economic Incentives**   78
   **Business Maximization Behavior**   78
   **Social Costs**   79
   **Profit and Market Structure**   79
   **Investment and Economic Growth**   80
   **Sources of Savings**   80

**LIST OF ECONOMIC UNDERSTANDINGS IN CONCEPT AREA IV**   81

**TEACHING APPLICATIONS IN CONCEPT AREA IV**   82

   **University Level Instruction**   82

      1. A Corporation is Formed: Simulation   82
      2. The Multiplier in Action   84
      3. Baldicer   88

   **Secondary Level Instruction**   89

      1. Duopoly   89
      2. Running a Snow Shoveling Business   91

   **Elementary Level Instruction**   95

      1. How About A Kool-Aid Stand   95

**EVALUATION INSTRUMENT OF CONCEPT AREA IV**   97

## Overview of Concept Area IV

**ECONOMIC INCENTIVES.** The motivational dimension of the market system can be found in the two basic assumptions on which the system is based. The first assumption deals with consumer behavior. It basically states that consumers as rational individuals will attempt to maximize their *utility* (well-being) by allocating limited income among the various available consumption alternatives in a fashion that will allow them to achieve the highest possible level of economic well being. The second assumption deals with the behavior of producers. It states that producers will allocate the various factors of production, that they can afford to purchase, in the most efficient possible manner so as to minimize the cost of producing a product or service and thus make the highest possible *profit*. If either of these two assumptions is violated then the market system will fail to achieve the desired efficiency that guarantees that the economy will allocate its scarce resources in a manner that will satisfy the greatest amount of its unlimited wants. If it weren't for profits, entrepreneurs would not be willing to take risks, to be efficient, to respond to consumer demand, and to innovate and expand their production capacity. More importantly, however, profits motivate producers to compete with each other, which results in lower prices for the consumer and, ironically, lower profits.

**BUSINESS MAXIMIZATION BEHAVIOR.** Each business firm will seek to produce at the *lowest possible cost*. A businessperson selling at any given market price can, by lowering costs, make more profit or diminish his or her loss. To lower costs, businesspeople continuously seek: (1) more efficient techniques of prodution; (2) less expensive combinations of factors that can produce their commodity, and (3) a more efficient level or size of production. Each businessperson will attempt to operate at the point where total revenue from sales is farthest above the total cost of production. Another way of looking at this optimum output level is where the revenue from the last unit sold just equals the cost of the last unit produced. (Until that production point, every unit adds more revenue than cost.) This analysis refers to the cost on the margin as marginal cost compared to revenue at the marginal revenue. The *profit maximizing point* is the point at which marginal costs is equal to marginal revenue. This point is reached when marginal costs increase with increased production and marginal revenue decreases with the lower price for a larger volume of sales.

If a business firm can produce a product more efficiently than its competitors, i.e., by reducing the cost of production, the firm may continue to sell its product at the same price of competing firms thereby making greater profits. Under some circumstances the more efficient firm may reduce its price to take business away from his competitors, and thereby increase profits. These greater profits, regardless of which decision is made, are usually realized for a relatively short period of time as other businesses adopt the lower cost methods. Competition between businesses, if effective, drives the price down to new levels and results in the elimination of business "extra" profits with only "normal" profits being realized. *Normal profit* is the minimum return or payment necessary to retain an entrepreneur in some specific line of production, whereas, *extra profits* are any profits realized in excess of normal profits. Thus, effective competition wipes out temporary large profit margins, lowers the price to consumers and forces the remaining businesses to adopt the efficient technique of production. Firms that cannot keep up with and continually adjust to improved and low cost methods of production are eliminated by losses as their successful competitors drive the price down. Competition is the fundamental regulator of the market system guaranteeing that resources will be allocated in the most optimum fashion and prices related to the costs of production.

**SOCIAL COSTS.** The manufacturer's cost of producing each product may not cover all hidden costs and these costs are not included in the commodity price; rather, are borne involuntarily by the rest of society. A common example is the smoke and dirt produced by some industrial plants. These costs are called *"social costs"* which must be cleaned up by society.

**PROFIT AND MARKET STRUCTURE.** The United States market economy consists of a mixture of industries characterized by varying degrees of competition. The phrase *market structure* refers to the degree of competition prevailing in a particular market and the extent to which the government intervenes in the market to influence the pricing process and the rate of profit. An example of a very competitive industry is agriculture. There are many produces producing virtually the same product in a very well organized market where information on prices is readily available to any buyer. On the other end of the spectrum the public utility companies are the only suppliers (monopolies) of electrical power, natural gas and telephone services in their geographical areas. Since competition is non existent the government imposes regulations on these companies to guarantee that the companies generate only a "normal" rate of profit and no "extra" profits are realized. Some industries in the U.S. have fewer producers than others due to the high cost of the technology and the need for a high volume of production to justify the cost. This results in only a few producers being able to satisfy the existing market demand; an example would be the automobile industry. Therefore, the economy is confronted with the job of maintaining a balance between production efficiency that large firms often make possible and the lack of competition where there are only a few firms may cause.

**INVESTMENT AND ECONOMIC GROWTH.** In order for an economy to continue to grow, and thus for its citizens to achieve a higher standard of living, it is necessary to produce more goods and services so that real income will increase. The first step in this process of *economic growth* is for the saving to take place. To an economist, saving is defined as the act of not consuming some of the resources available for consumption. The second step is to direct these saved resources to the production of capital goods; which is the act of *investment*. Capital goods are tangible human made items, such as machinery, buildings and equipment that are used to produce other goods. Capital goods are required for economic growth in order to make the labor force more productive and to realize the efficiencies of mass production. Therefore before any investment can take place, saving has to occur.

**SOURCE OF SAVINGS.** *Savings* in a market economy are either provided by households or by business. *Household savings* are allocated by the financial institutions to business, government and to other households who pay the original savers a rate of interest in exchange for the use of their saved resources. Therefore it becomes apparent that not all savings are directed towards investment, rather, a growing portion is used by other households and government for consumption purposes. Some of the government borrowing, however, is directed toward investment in the economy's infrastructure for items such as highways and dams. *Business savings* are largely in the form of past profits that were not distributed to the owners of the business when they were earned, but were retained by the business for investment purposes. A growing number of large corporations use this method to finance their investment and thus their future growth instead of borrowing from outside sources. Corporations, however, can issue common stock, preferred stock or bonds in order to raise funds directly from the individual savers. Other business forms, the single proprietorships and partnerships, have to depend more on financial institutions for their investment funds.

# LIST OF ECONOMIC UNDERSTANDINGS IN CONCEPT AREA IV

1. The market system will function properly only if customers and producers maximize their own economic well-being. This could be achieved by the consumer maximizing utility and the producer maximizing profit.

2. To maximize profit a producer of goods will increase output to the point where the cost of the increment of increase output just equals the revenue (income) from the sale of the same increment of increased output.

3. A "social cost" is a cost not covered by the manufacturer and therefore not included in the selling price of the product. Such costs are borne involuntarily by the society in general.

4. If competition prevails in a market "extra" profits will tend to be eliminated and producers will tend to earn "normal" profits.

5. "Normal" profits are the minimum return or payment necessary to retain an entrepreneur in some specific line of production; "extra" profits are any profits realized in excess of normal profits.

6. The U.S. market economy is characterized as having a mixture of industries with competition in differing degrees.

7. Some industries in the U.S. have fewer producers due to the nature of the technology available to produce the product; such industries often require a high volume of production in relation to the limitations of their markets.

8. Saving is defined as the act of not consuming some of the resources available for consumption.

9. Saving is the precondition of investment. Investment is the act of transforming saved resources into capital goods.

10. Captial goods and investment in human capital are necessary for economic growth.

11. Financial institutions direct saved resources to the available investment opportunities in order to generate economic growth.

12. Some corporations finance their expansions, i.e., investment, through their own savings; others tap household savings by issuing common stock, preferred stock or bonds.

# TEACHING APPLICATIONS IN CONCEPT AREA IV

## University Level Instruction

**A Corporation is Formed: Simulation**

The student will be able to understand that:

> *Primary Economic Understanding:* A growing business will sell shares of ownership in order to get money for expansion for which they will issue shares of stock.
>
> *Secondary Economic Understanding:* Investment bankers will pay cash for the stock and sell it to the public.

*Purpose:* This activity will familiarize students with a procedure for raising capital for expansion which becomes a part of economic growth of the economy.

*Materials and Instruction:*

1. Use the article as a basis for a simulation in which students will role play this story.
2. Students may choose a class project for the simulation or a Jr. Achievement project.

*Economic Content and Debriefing:*

1. This is a new issue of stock simulation and it is sold by investment bankers, in contrast to the stock that has been previously sold and circulated on the Stock Exchange.
2. The new issue of stock represents an accumulation of money for investment in the business for expansion and economic growth.

This fictional story of the JOHNSON GAGE CORPORATION is an example of capitalism — sometimes called the "free enterprise system," "the individual enterprise system," or the "free economy." Under this system any person has the right to own and transfer property, start a business, make a profit, and work on a job of his own choice. In other words, control of economic activities rests primarily in the hands of private individuals like you and me. This kind of economy — capitalism, or free

## Profits, Savings and Economic Growth 83

enterprise — has proved to be very successful in our country. For instance, the United States produces about $1/3$ of all goods and services produced in the world, although it has only about $1/17$ of the world's population.

Sid Johnson had always been interested in radio and electronics. Sid spent his spare time dabbling with stereo sets — experimenting with different combinations of parts made by various companies.

Sid's friends liked his sets so much they asked him to build sets for them. Demand for sets began to pile up. Sid decided to give up his job in the printing plant and go into the business of making and repairing stereo sets. He advertised in the local newspaper, calling his business JOHNSON'S HI-FI HOUSE. Sid was the sole owner, or proprietor. He paid all expenses: for materials and equipment, rent for his small shop, taxes, advertising. The profits — the money left over after paying all expenses, including taxes — belonged to him and to no one else.

Two years later he decided to form a partnership with George Gage, who provided enough money so that together they could build their own shop and buy labor-saving tools and machinery. Of course, they turned out more stereo sets than Sid alone could, and they divided both the expenses and profits.

The business continued to grow. In three years Sid and George could not keep up with the demand for their sets, although they had employed six people to help assemble the sets and build the cabinets. The partners realized they would have to expand to keep up with the demand for their products and maybe increase their profits. Expansion would mean a larger plant, more machinery, tools and employees, including salesman. Through their research efforts they had discovered how to build or assemble some parts — such as amplifiers and speakers — more cheaply and better than those they were buying from other manufacturers. This production, however, would require complicated and expensive machinery plus more workers.

The partners needed about $500,000 to expand, far more money than they could put up themselves or wanted to borrow. They decided the way to get the money was to let some other people become owners with them. So they set up the JOHNSON GAGE CORPORATION under the laws of their state. Now they needed to get people to buy shares of ownership in their new *corporation*. These share-buyers would provide the money for the expansion. They turned to an *investment banking firm,* one that specializes in raising money needed to start or expand businesses. Such money is called *capital.*

The investment bankers carefully investigated the new corporation. They decided it was sound and that its products would sell. So they paid cash for some of the *common stock* in the JOHNSON GAGE CORPORATION. A total of 60,000 shares of stock represented the ownership of the corporation. Sid and George transferred their partnership business (including the factory, machinery, tools, customers and good will) to the new corporation for 10,000 shares of the stock. The bankers bought the remaining 50,000.

The price of the newly issued stock was determined by the investment bankers and the JOHNSON GAGE CORPORATION. Since $500,000 was needed, they decided to sell the 50,000 shares at a price of $10 per share to the investment bankers. However, they could have issued more stock, say, 500,000 shares, and sold it at $1 per share.

After complying with federal and state regulations relating to the sale of stock, the investment bankers sold the 50,000 shares to the public at a price higher than $10 per share. This is the way the investment bankers make their profit. The process of having an investment banking firm buy stock of a corporation and then sell the stock later to the public is called *underwriting*.

Since ownership of the corporation was now represented by 60,000 shares of stock, Sid and George with 10,000 shares owned 1/6 of the business:

$$\frac{10,000}{60,000} = 1/6$$

Anyone with 100 shares would own 1/600th of the corporation.

With the JOHNSON GAGE CORPORATION, as with any publicly owned corporation, the ownership may be constantly changing as its stock is bought and sold by the public. The liquidity of stock — the ease of buying and selling — is important for any investor to consider. When a person buys a stock he likes to know that he can convert it to cash if necessary and advisable.

This is only ONE way small businesses can grow into large businesses — by changing from a proprietorship into a partnership and eventually into a corporation. There is, however, no set pattern. Sometimes businesses start as corporations with many share-owners supplying a lot of money, called *venture capital*. Such businesses are large from the beginning.

This process of getting money from private individuals to finance businesses is an every day practice in the United States. It is a basic feature of our capitalistic economic system. With this money, or capital, the corporation buys machinery, tools, and materials, builds factories, creates new jobs, and develops new products.

**The Multiplier In Action***

The student will be able to understand that:

> *Primary Economic Understanding:* A change in expenditures results in an increase in the total income that is greater than the initial increase.

---

*Economics. Cooperative Research Program. Ohio University. Meno Lovenstein.

## Profits, Savings and Economic Growth

*Secondary Economic Understanding:* The multiple effect of a change in total expenditures as the result of an initial change in expenditures is called the multiplier effect. The effect is determined by (1) the size of the original change and (2) the tendencies of consumers to spend and save.

*Purpose:* The students will use this activity to understand the multiplier effect. Because they have worked with the project, they will understand that these positive results originate with the amount saved.

*Materials and Instructions:*
1. Students may use this project as desk work or may develop a similar money-making project for which they will keep records and calculate the amount of Income to Clubs, Consumption Expenditures and Savings by the Club.
2. Students will be asked to read the introductory paragraph that explains the project; given the set of information, ask the students to work through these projects. Determine the size of the multiplier. Change the amount of savings and tell how it affected the size of the multiplier.
3. Have the students read through the following:

### The Multiplier

The Student Council of Central High School was holding its biweekly meeting when the representative of the Student Athletic Council announced that his club had received $100 as its share of the proceeds from ticket sales at athletic events. The Athletic Council had decided it needed a new ticket booth and were willing to pay the Industrial Arts Club $80 to build it. This was an offer the Industrial Arts Club could not reject. The Industrial Arts Club had just given an exhibition of its projects and had asked the Photography Club to shoot pictures of it. For all the photographic work, the printing and framing of the pictures, the Industrial Arts club paid the Photography Club $51.20. The photographers had to have the frames for the pictures made by the Art Club, and they paid $41 for these frames. The Art Club in turn paid the School Newspaper $32.80 to have several pages of their artwork published in the paper. The remaining money was received and spent among the various clubs in the school. Each of these transactions became successively smaller and smaller in amount. For example, one of the last few transactions was the cheerleaders' purchase of ten cents worth of confetti from the school store.

## Profits, Savings and Economic Growth

The table below follows the flow of income generated by the original $100.

| Period | Income to Clubs | Consumption Expenditures | Savings by Clubs |
|---|---|---|---|
| 0 | 0 | 0 | 0 |
| 1. Student Athletic Council | $100.00 | $ 80.00 | $ 20.00 |
| to | | | |
| 2. Industrial Arts Club | 80.00 | 64.00 | 16.00 |
| to | | | |
| 3. Photography Club | 64.00 | 51.20 | 12.80 |
| to | | | |
| 4. Art Club | 51.20 | 41.00 | 10.20 |
| to | | | |
| 5. School Newspaper | 41.00 | 32.80 | 8.20 |
| 6 | 32.80 | 26.20 | 6.60 |
| 7 | 26.20 | 21.00 | 5.20 |
| 8 | 21.00 | 16.80 | 4.20 |
| 9 | 16.80 | 13.40 | 3.40 |
| 10 | 13.40 | 10.70 | 2.70 |
| 11 | 10.70 | 8.60 | 2.10 |
| 12 | 8.60 | 6.90 | 1.70 |
| 13 | 6.90 | 5.50 | 1.40 |
| 14 | 5.50 | 4.40 | 1.10 |
| 15 | 4.40 | 3.50 | .90 |
| . | . | . | . |
| All other Periods | 17.50 | 14.00 | 3.50 |
| Totals | $500.00 | $400.00 | $100.00 |

**Question:** How much money from outside the Student Council came into the funds of this group?

**Answer:** $100—The original income from the sale of tickets at athletic events.

**Question:** How much money was saved through the whole series of transactions among the clubs at Central High?

**Answer:** $100 — In the first transaction the Athletic Council saved $20 of its income of $100, in the second transaction the

### Profits, Savings and Economic Growth

Industrial Arts Club saved $16, in the third transaction the Photography Club saved $13.80, The Art club saved $10.20 and the Newspaper saved $8.20 and so on till all transactions were completed. The total savings was $100.

**Question:** From the original $100 earned by the Athletic Council, how much income was created for all the clubs of the school?

**Answer:** $500—The Athletic Council earned $100 selling tickets, the Industrial Arts Club, $80 for building a new ticket booth, the Photography Club $64 for its work, the Art Club received $51.20 from the Photography Club, the Newspaper earned $41 for services to the Art Club, and so on till the total reached $500.

As was shown in the table above and the questions and answers which followed the table, the change of expenditure of $100 created by the income from ticket sales resulted in a total increase in income of all the groups in the school of $500. This example shows the multiple effect of a change in the level of expenditures. This effect, called *the multiplier,* is determined by (1) the size of the original change in expenditures and (2) the tendencies of consumers to spend and save. The amount of additional income which is used to buy goods and services is known as the *marginal propensity to consume* or MPC, and the amount saved is referred to as the *marginal propensity to save* or MPS. The MPS is determined by subtracting MPC from the total disposable income. MPS is sometimes referred to as the leakage from total income. These terms are used in determining the multiplier. The formula for the multiplier is:

$$\text{multiplier} = \frac{1}{1-\text{MPC}}$$

For example:

(1) In the case of Central High School, 80% of income was spent (MPC) in each of the transactions leaving 20% leakage (MPS). When leakage is 1/5 (20%) expressed as a fraction,

then the multiplier = $\frac{1}{1-4/5} = \frac{1}{1/5} = 5$.

(2) If the MPC=75% and MPS=25% or 1/4,
then the multiplier will be $\frac{1}{1-3/4} = \frac{1}{1/4} = 4$.

(3) Determine the size of the multiplier when:
    (a) MPC = 66 2/3%  (Answer:  3)
    (b) MPS = 50%  (Answer:  2)

*Economic Content and Debriefing:*

1. The multiplier will vary in different groups in society. The size of the multiplier is determined by the size of savings.

2. The multiplier effect is the result of individuals spending and saving their income. Group I saves part and spends part of the income with Group B. Group B spends part of the money spent by A, and saves the rest. The increased expenditures represent additional transactions that become a part of economic growth with a multiplier effect.

3. The amount of growth, depression or inflation experienced by the economy will be determined by the magnitude of the chain reaction. When all the reactions are considered, a multiple effect can be seen as the result of an initial change in the magnitude of expenditures by one or more sectors. This effect is known as the multiplier.

**Baldicer***

The student will be able to understand that:

> *Primary Economic Understanding:* The more resources a society has access to, the higher will be the standard of living it will be able to achieve.
>
> *Secondary Economic Understandings:* Saving is the act of not consuming some of the resources available for consumption.
>
> Saving is the precondition for investment. Investment is the act of transforming saved resources into capital goods. Capital goods are necessary for economic growth.

*Purpose:* This simulation places the students in a position of responsibility for feeding the population of their country. Each country is given a specific amount of resources to start with. Most countries start with barely enough to sustain their populations whereas only two countries will hold the key to survival of the world as they will have enough resources to save and invest in capital goods or machines which are the engines of development.

*Materials and Instructions:* This is a commercially produced game that can be purchased from the publisher. It consists of student instructions, work sheets with different given endowments and an instructor's manual. Each round of the game takes the students through producing their food, trading with other countries and making their decisions on the allocation of their resources between consumption, saving and investment.

---
*Baldicer: A Simulation Game on Feeding the World's Population* by Georgeann Wilcoxson, John Knox Press, Richmond, Virginia, 1970.

*Economic Content and Debriefing:*

1. The countries of the world are not endowed with the same amount of resources, but rather each country has its own special blend of resources. This point could be supplemented by selecting a few countries with different resource endowments such as Australia, Israel, Saudi Arabia and Bangladesh and ask the students to compare their resources.

2. It is not enough for a country to be rich for it to achieve a high standard of living. However, the richer the country the greater its ability to save and thus invest. The point that the simulation makes very clear is that even the rich countries have to purchase machines in order to be able to increase their standard of living.

3. As some countries fail to feed their population and perish, the rich countries will have to make the decision of whether to help them survive or not. This is a very relevant issue in today's world as on the one hand the poor countries of the world are seeking to have world resources distributed in a manner that they feel is more equitable. On the other hand, the rich countries of the world have to make sacrifices, i.e., reduce their own level of consumption in order to provide the poor countries with foreign aid.

## Secondary Level Instruction

### Duopoly*

The student will be able to understand that:

> *Primary Economic Understanding:* If competition prevails in a market "extra" profits will be eliminated and producers will earn "normal" profits.
>
> *Secondary Economic Understandings:* "Normal" profits are the minimum return or payment necessary to retain an entrepreneur in some specific line of production; "extra" profits are profits realized in excess of normal profits.
>
> The smaller the number of producers of a particular product, the easier it is for them to collude and maintain a relatively higher price in the market.

*Purpose:* This simulation is used to show the student the interdependence of producers in a duopoly or oligopoly market.

---

*Duopoly* is adapted from "Oligopoly and Merger: A Simple Classroom Game" by Richard A. Miller, *The Journal of Economic Education*, Volume 2, number 2., 1971, pp. 142-150.

# Profits, Savings and Economic Growth

*Materials and Instructions:*

1. Divide the class into two groups. Select a leadership team from each group to make the decision of the two firms involved in the market.

2. Either reproduce the following table and distribute it to each member of the class to do their own calculations or select a few students to do the calculations on the chalkboard.

|  | 1 | 2 | 3 | 4 | 5 | 6 | 7 | 8 | 9 |  |  |
|---|---|---|---|---|---|---|---|---|---|---|---|
| Quantity |  |  |  |  |  |  |  |  |  |  |  |
| Total Cost |  |  |  |  |  |  |  |  |  |  |  |
| Price |  |  |  |  |  |  |  |  |  |  |  |
| Total Revenue |  |  |  |  |  |  |  |  |  |  |  |
| Profit |  |  |  |  |  |  |  |  |  |  |  |

3. The class should understand that each firm is independent of the other firm. Both firms have equal costs of $2. They produce an identical product and there will be no new entry into the market. Both firms know the demand schedule for the product. No storage of the product is allowed and both firms prefer more profit to less profit.

4. Each firm should then make its output decisions independently and then combine both outputs to figure out the market price for the product. The price times the quantity produced by each firm gives the total revenue for the period, and the average cost times the quantity results in the total cost. The difference between total revenue and total cost results in profit.

5. Allow each firm to change its output in each time period and determine its profit.

*Economic Content and Debriefing:*

1. The monopoly or cartel price is where Marginal Cost equals Price at $2. This will result from a quantity of 98 units. This quantity will result in

maximum possible combined profit for the market. As the class proceeds in the simulation they will realize the profit maximizing point and probably develop some sort of tacit or informal agreement to split the market between them. This shows that producers do not need to communicate with each other in order to monopolize the market but rather can reach that stage through independent actions.

2. Allow the formation of more firms in that market in order to see the effect of competition on output and thus the price. The demand schedule could be easily adjusted to accomodate more than two firms. The results should be similar to the first round of the game with only two firms except that the larger the number of firms, the longer it will take for the interdependence to be realized and the informal agreement to develop. As the number of producers increases the benefits of cheating on the informal agreement also increases. This results in a larger level of output and lower prices.

3. An existing or new firm may have an innovation and enter the competitive market.

**Running a Snow Shoveling Business***

The student will be able to understand that:

*Primary Economic Understanding:* Capital goods are necessary for economic growth.

*Secondary Economic Understanding:* Financial institutions direct saved resources to the available investment opportunities in order to generate economic growth.

Saving is the precondition of investment. Investment is the act of transforming saved resources into capital goods.

*Purpose:* This simulation demonstrates to the student the importance of capital goods in the production process. It also allows the student to face the various uncertainties that a typical firm would face.

*Materials and Instructions:*

1. Duplicate the instruction sheet and the tally sheet and distribute to each student.

---
*This simulation was developed by Louise M. Vertal of the Cleveland Public School System.

## 92   Profits, Savings and Economic Growth

2. Provide each student with a card or paper representing ownership of a snow shovel, snow blower or a snow plow. (The student has only one of the above at a time.)
3. During each round provide the number of snow days. Round one is 5 days, round two is 4 days, round three is 6 days, round four is 5 days, round five is 4 days.
4. Make out risk or transaction cards which read as follows and are used at the correct time in the simulation:

Enter one risk per card.

   a. Equipment breaks. If you own a shovel, repairs are $6.00; if you own a blower repairs are $50.00; if you own a plow repairs are $100.00.
   b. Ran out of rock salt—replace at $5.00.
   c. Get customer tips of $15.00.
   d. Taxes due—pay $15.00 if you own a shovel; pay $30.00 if you own a blower and pay $75.00 if you own a plow.
   e. Get tax rebate of $15.00 if you own a shovel; $30.00 if you own a blower and $75.00 if you own a plow.
   f. Donate $15.00 to the United Torch.
   g. Customer complains you did a poor job. Refund money of $10.00 if you own a shovel; $20.00 if you own a blower; $50.00 if you own a plow.
   h. If you lowered your price in this round, you get 3 more customers. If you own a shovel add $15.00; if you own a blower add $30.00; if you own a plow add $75.00.
   i. If you raised your price in this round, you lost 3 customers. If you own a shovel subtract $15.00; if you own a blower substract $30.00; if you own a plow subtract $75.00.

5. Each student needs paper and pencil for the work activity.
6. Student Instructions:

The objective of this simulation will be to operate a single proprietorship in a snow shoveling business, in order to make as much money as you can. The winner is the one with the most profit.

You need capital goods and savings to start the business. Money will be borrowed from a Savings and Loan Company. There is simple interest of 10% charged on the loan. A contract is signed requiring payment of the loan in the final round of play.

## Profits, Savings and Economic Growth      93

After the contract has been signed, play begins with a period of work activity. This work activity is a writing of the words "SLIPPERY, SLIDING, SLUSH, SNOW" as many times as you can in 60 seconds. This number of times written is placed on the tally sheet. This tally sheet becomes a form of business ledger in which you will figure out the profits and losses. There will be six rounds of play representing six business weeks.

Once the work activity score is entered on the tally sheet, the figure is multiplied by 1 if you own a snow shovel, by 2 if you own a snow blower or by 5 if you own a snow plow. Each week it shows a different number of days. The leader of the game provides you with this information. It is placed on the appropriate line on the tally sheet. Products are taken and recorded in the places on the tally sheet. The amount you charge a customer in the first round is $2.00. This amount can be changed by you any way you wish after that round. Each player takes a product depending on the amount charged. You then must take a Business Card and do what the card says on the appropriate line of the tally sheet. These cards represent risk to the owners of single proprietorships. A total is taken. Then the balance from the previous round is added in. Transaction time of about ten minutes is given for you to purchase a snow blower for $200.00 or a snow plow for $500.00. A trade-in value of $10.00 is given you if you trade-in a blower for a snow plow. During the transaction time you may borrow more money or make other deals with other players.

*RULES:* *

a. You borrow the capital from the Savings and Loan. The shovel costs $13.00 and rock salt $5.00. The simple interest is $1.80. This is paid back in the final round.

b. You write the words "SLIPPERY, SLIDING, SLUSH, SNOW" only when told to for 60 seconds.

c. You can only own one snow shovel, snow blower or snow plow at a time.

d. Snow blowers and plows can only be purchased from the leader during the transaction time. It is used in the next round.

e. Snow blowers cost $200. and increase production by 2 times; snow plows cost $500 or $400 with a trade-in of a blower and increase production by 5 times.

*A second round can be played to show the effect of doubling the level of savings.

## 94   Profits, Savings and Economic Growth

f. You must show a profit or a balance of 0 in order to continue to the next round.

g. If you go bankrupt, you can not play the next round unless you come up with the money needed for a 0 balance. You can borrow more money from the Savings and Loan at 20% simple interest or you can make any deal with another student.

h. The amount charged a customer in round one is $2.00. It can be raised only by 50¢ in each round. It can be lowered any way you wish.

## SAVINGS AND LOAN CONTRACT

I, _____ agree to borrow $18.00 at a rate of 10% simple interest in the amount of $1.80. The total amount to be borrowed is $19.80. This will be repaid during the sixth week of business. *

Signature of the borrower _____

Signature of the creditor _____

\*    \*    \*    \*    \*    \*    \*    \*    \*    \*    \*    \*    \*

---

*The interest rate can be adjusted for current conditions.

## TALLY SHEET

| Rounds | 1 | 2 | 3 | 4 | 5 | 6 |
|---|---|---|---|---|---|---|
| 1. enter work score | | | | | | |
| 2. multiply by 1 if you have a shovel, by 2 if you have a blower, or by 5 if you have a plow. | XI | | | | | |
| 3. product of 1 x 2 | | | | | | |
| 4. number of snow days | | | | | | |
| 5. product of 3 x 4 | | | | | | |
| 6. amount charged | | | | | | |
| 7. product of 5 x 6 | | | | | | |
| 8. Business Card add or subtract | | | | | | |
| 9. Total of 8 & 7 | | | | | | |
| 10. Add amount of previous round (balance) | — | | | | | |
| 11. Total of 9 & 10 | | | | | | |
| 12. Transaction Time (buy blower or plow or make any deal) | | | | | | |
| 13. Pay back loan | — | — | — | — | — | -19.80 |
| 14. Final total of round. | | | | | | |

## Elementary Level Instruction

### Let's Go Into Business: How About a Kool-Aid Stand

The students will understand that:

*Primary Economic Understanding:* Profit is the compensation paid to the enterpreneur who combines the other three factors of production to produce a product.

*Secondary Economic Understanding:* Savings is the main source of capital. Every business needs capital in order to start and to grow. Competition will eliminate "extra profits." "Normal" profits is the minimum return or payment to retain an enterpreneur in a specific line of production.

## 96  Profits, Savings and Economic Growth

*Purpose:* This activity develops the awareness of the elementary student of the various requirements for starting a business.

*Materials and Instructions:*

1. Write on different cards the various steps involved in setting up a Kool-Aid stand. They could look as follows:
    a. Earn or borrow money to pay for the Kool-Aid, the cups, etc. . . .
    b. Make ice cubes.
    c. Make a sign.
    d. Set a table and two chairs to tend store.
    e. Wash an empty gallon jug.
    f. Make the Kool-Aid.
    g. Sit down and sell Kool-Aid, but don't forget to smile.
2. Write the sequence number on the back of each card.
3. Shuffle the cards and have the students put them in the correct sequence.
4. If the students wish to apply their learning by recording their expenses, revenue and the difference between the two, they may determine the profit made at the Kool-Aid stand.
5. Ask the students about what will happen to their profit if every child in the neighborhood had his own Kool-Aid stand, and compare it to the situation if only one did.

*Economic Content and Debriefing:*

1. Setting up a business is an involved process that requires preparation, market analysis and an adequate amount of knowledge and savings.

2. The gallon jug, table and chairs are the capital goods that are used in producing other goods. The more capital goods that are available the larger the amount of output possible.

3. The more competition in the market, i.e. the more Kool-Aid sellers, the lower profit will be. "Extra profits" (dollar return to the owners greater than the amount necessary to maintain production) will be eliminated. As profits decline due to increased competition these stands with costs above their competitors may be forced to close down.

4. Normal profits are the minimum amount of return that will keep the Kool-Aid stand in business. This acceptable minimum return or payment to the factors of production (materials, labor, risk takers of savings for initial capital, and equipment) depends on the available alternative uses for those factors of production.

In this case, the comparative opportunity of income to the factors of production in the Kool-Aid stand determines the minimum amount of return that will keep the Kool-Aid stand in business.

# EVALUATION OF CONCEPT AREA IV

1. Compare the desire of the consumer to maximize utility with the desire of the producer to maximize profits.

2. Describe the process by which a firm attempts to maximize its profits.

3. Why are profits necessary in a market economy?

4. What services are rendered by the fourth factor of production? What is the form of payment to the fourth factor of production?

5. Differentiate between a "normal" profit and an "extra" profit.

6. Explain why "extra" profits in a highly competitive market, would tend to be temporary. How are the extra profits eliminated?

7. How can the desire for corporate profits actually lead to lower prices for the consumer.

8. Evaluate the alternative ways available to a corporation to finance an expansion of plant capacity.

9. Why is the American economy characterized by industries of varying degrees of competition?

10. Why are there only a few firms in some profitable industries?

11. Explain why saving is the first step to economic growth.

12. What role do capital goods play in improving the standard of living of the people of a society?

For reference, use List of Economic Understandings for this Concept Area.

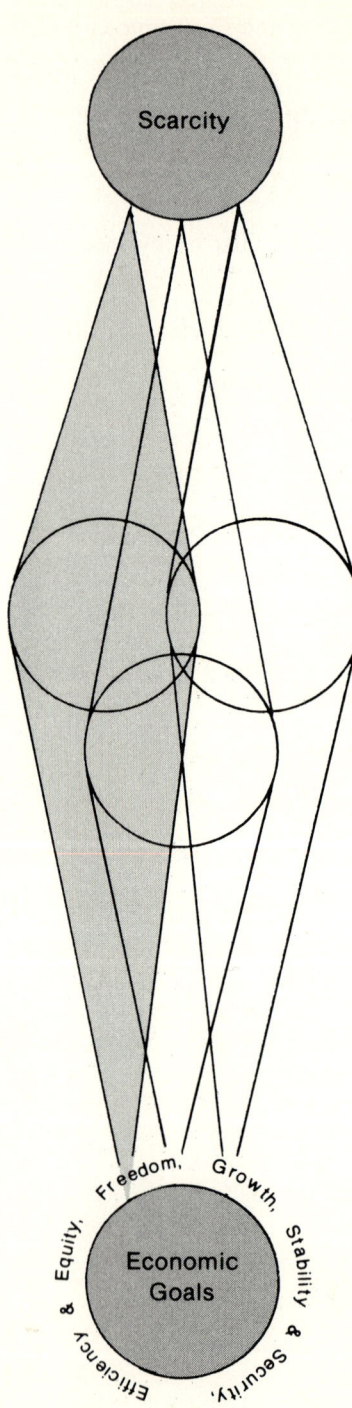

● -Personal and Household Finance (Spending and savings program of the household.)

Complete code of screenings for Model on Page 6.

# CONSUMER SPENDING AND SAVING

## Concept Area V

## Contents

**OVERVIEW OF CONCEPT AREA V**    100

  **Consumer Problems**    100
  **Consumer Opportunity Costs**    100
  **Consumer Budgeting and Shopping**    100
  **Consumer Saving and Investing**    101
  **Consumer Credit**    101

**LIST OF ECONOMIC UNDERSTANDINGS IN CONCEPT AREA V**    102

**TEACHING APPLICATIONS IN CONCEPT AREA V**    103

  **University Level Instruction**    103

    1. The Budget Game    103
    2. Investment Decisions    104
    3. The Money Management IQ    105
    4. The Monthly Cost Question    106

  **Secondary Level Instruction**    108

    1. Consumer Goals/Opportunity Cost    108
    2. Hidden Costs    110

  **Elementary Level Instruction**    110

    1. Comparative Shopping    110
    2. The Potato Chip Game    112

**EVALUATION INSTRUMENT OF CONCEPT AREA V**    114

## OVERVIEW OF CONCEPT AREA V

**CONSUMER PROBLEMS.** The consumer goal is to obtain maximum satisfaction from his or her available resources. Economic Well-Being = Personal Resources × Individual Affluency. Family financial management is organized spending and saving geared to a family's way of life. The plan should be reached by mutual agreement of family members. This planning permits the family to think of alternative living plans and therefore helps to clarify, to appraise and to put in priority personal goals and values. These can be worked into short-term intermediate and long-term goals. Goals are best handled by establishing a personal time plan; then at regular intervals, reviewing actual conduct against the plan. The consumer has specific and personal problems to consider:

- *Intelligent budgeting and buying*
- *Appropriate savings and investment*
- *Alternative credit forms and their costs*

**CONSUMER OPPORTUNITY COSTS.** The principle of *opportunity or alternative costs* is important in analyzing buying and budgeting problems. The principle is that for any item individual consumers might purchase, they must consider if there is any other item they could buy which would bring more satisfaction. For example, in adding all costs of owning and operating a washer, all implicit (opportunity) and explict costs should be calculated to compare all benefits. The explicit costs are the out-of-pocket costs; the implicit costs are those forgone opportunities such as the investing of the money spent for the washer in alternative investments to earn a return. (The forgone opportunity or implicit cost can be calculated by taking the value of the washer times the available interest rate.)

**CONSUMER BUDGETING AND SHOPPING.** An individual family budget should be tailored to the family goals; however, it does help to know how other people live and divide their incomes. A typical household in the USA spends about 40% of its budget on housing, 20% on food, 15% on clothing, personal and medical care and the remaining 25% on transportation, education, recreation and savings.

A careful shopper is not an impulse buyer; does not expect something for nothing; does not buy high fashion that is quickly out-of-date merchandise; does not consistently charge purchases and does not shop uninformed. That same careful shopper will make a plan for large expenditures; will buy in quantities with the lowest cost per unit; will read labels and guarantees; will consider time and energy as well as money and will exercise the right of protest, if needed.

**CONSUMER SAVING AND INVESTING.** Americans save between 6%-7% of their disposable income. These savings may be put in savings and loan associations, in banks, in life insurance companies, in bonds, in stocks, in real estate, in investment companies, and in credit unions. Individuals save in order to provide for incomes during periods of reduced income, such as sickness or retirement. The higher the interest paid and the higher the variability of income, the more is saved. Savings are, in turn, loaned by banks to individuals and businesses for purchasing capital goods; capital investment generally prompts efficiency, increased profits and general economic growth.

A good *personal investment* plan will include: (a) necessary insurance, (b) an emergency fund equal to one-half to one year's salary, (c) purchases for personal needs such as a home or business, and (d) a general fund. Some of the factors which investors should consider are the amount of return, the risk involved, and the liquidity (ease with which the investment can be converted into cash.) Investment means the exchange of money for bonds, stocks, real estate, etc., with the hope of a rise in value of its income. Insurance may provide protection and investment opportunity; however the two are quite different, and the investment portion should be considered separately for comparison with other investment opportunities. All schemes to "get rich quick" should be investigated thoroughly; rarely will any such scheme guarantee you a higher than normal rate of return without a higher amount risk.

**CONSUMER CREDIT.** Individuals borrow for necessity, for convenience, and to increase their standard of living. Individual borrowing often requires a systematic spending program which will provide that individual with the opportunity to consume goods and services that he or she would not otherwise be able to consume. Installment payments on debt, often entered into to obtain service of a large item without paying for it all at once, can be thought of as matching the service flow of the good or service. Considerations in the *granting of credit* include: (a) character—history of payment of accounts in the past, (b) capacity—earning ability or income, (c) capital—the economic goods that are owned by the person desiring credit and (d) conditions—the conditions of the economy at the time of the request. Interest is a price and a cost for borrowing money and should therefore be examined as carefully as any other price. The calculation of the interest charge, the compounding of interest if any and the time of crediting a payment should be determined and compared for alternative sources of credit. It is important to understand the different forms and costs of credit available to the consumer as well as the value of a good credit rating and the role of collateral.

# LIST OF ECONOMIC UNDERSTANDINGS IN CONCEPT AREA V

1. Individual Economic Well-Being = Personal Resources × Individual Affluence.

2. A spending and savings plan permits the family to think of alternative living plans and give priority to personal goals and values.

3. The principle of opportunity cost is important in analyzing buying and budgetary problems.

4. A typical household in the USA spends about 40% of its budget on housing, 20% on food, 15% on clothing, personal and medical care and the remaining 25% on transportation, education, recreation and savings.

5. A careful shopper considers many things such as quality, fashion changes, cost per unit, guarantees, and time and energy.

6. A good personal investment plan will include: (a) necessary insurance, (b) an emergency fund equal to one-half to one year's salary, (c) purchases for personal needs such as a home or business, and (d) a general fund.

7. Factors which investors should consider are the amount of return, the risk involved, and the liquidity of an investment.

8. Insurance may provide protection and investment opportunity. However the two are quite different and the investment portion should be considered separately from the protection aspect.

9. Credit depends on (a) character—history of payment of accounts in the past, (b) capacity—earning ability or income, (c) capital—economic goods that are owned by the person desiring credit and (d) conditions—conditions of the economy at the time of the request.

10. Alternative sources of credit should be examined for the interest charge, the compounding of interest and the time of crediting a payment.

# TEACHING APPLICATIONS IN CONCEPT AREA V

## University Level Instruction

**The Budget Game***

The students will be able to understand that:

> *Primary Economic Understanding:* A spending and saving plan permits the family to think of alternative living plans and personal goals and values in priority.
>
> *Secondary Economic Understandings:* A typical household in the USA spends about 40% of its budget on housing, 20% on food, 15% on clothing, personal and medical care and the remaining 25% on transportation, education, recreation and savings.
>
> The principle of opportunity cost is important in analyzing buying and budgetary problems.

*Purpose:* This simulation introduces students to family income budgeting in order to famiIarize them with the budgeting problems encountered by a typical family.

*Materials and Instructions:* This is a commercially produced game that can be purchased from the publisher. It consists of a budget worksheet, student instructions, monthly situation cards, and various commodities and services available for each family to purchase. The game is played by having each family make its choices on the selection of a residence, an automobile and luxury items. Each month or round the families have to determine their budget utilizing the worksheet and taking into account an unexpected item as presented by the situation cards.

*Economic Content and Debriefing:*

1. Each family has to stay within its allocated income thus each is faced with a set of choices. These choices involve compromises that are faced by most families in real life.

2. Each family will find that it needs some savings that is immediately accessible for emergencies.

---

*The Budget Game
Available from Changing Times Education Service, division of EMC Corporation, 180 East Sixth Street, St. Paul, Minnesota 55101.

3. The only borrowing allowed in this game is for purchasing a home or car. The game could be expanded to include borrowing for consumption purposes. This would add to the realism of the game.

4. There are minimum expenditures on basic needs such as food and shelter. This will limit the choices that each family can make.

**Investment Decisions**

The student will be able to understand that:

> *Primary Economic Understanding:* Income is apportioned according to major expenditures, and savings may be allocated among alternative investment opportunities for future consumption.
>
> *Secondary Economic Understanding:* Discussion for investments will be made according to the characteristics of different kinds of investments using the following criteria: risk, yield, liquidity, convenience.

*Purpose:* This exercise will help students become better spenders and savers by causing them to rank expenditures in the order of their importance and to evaluate investment alternatives by ranking the important characteristics of each investment opportunity.

*Materials and Instructions:*

> Each student should be given the following form and asked to rank expenditures 1 through 5 in the order of their importance; also to rank each element of investment (risk, yield, liquidity and convenience) for each investment 1 through 5. The number 1 is the highest level for that element and number 5 is the lowest level for the element.

### Expenditures and Savings

Give priority to each of the following items of expenditures and savings.

_____ Home
_____ Family Business
_____ Three-month reserve for emergencies
_____ Insurance
_____ Other
_____ Personal Investment Plan

| Investment | Risk | Yield | Liquidity | Convenience |
|---|---|---|---|---|
| Savings Account | | | | |
| Certificates of Deposit | | | | |
| Corporate Stocks | | | | |
| Bonds | | | | |
| Real Estate | | | | |
| Other | | | | |

*Economic Content and Debriefing:*

1. In spending, it is important first to provide for the unexpected by holding a dollar in reserve for emergencies; and thus securing a home before other Investment opportunities are considered.

2. Insurance is important to reduce the risk to any one person.

3. No one Investment has all desired characteristics in desired amounts.

4. All Investment opportunities have varying amounts of risk, yield, liquidity and convenience. It is important to establish one's personal priorities as to these investment characteristics.

5. Key to answers:

Key:   3, 4, 1, 2, (?), 5
         Risk 5, 4, 1, 3, 2,
         Yield 5, 4, 1, 3, 2,
         Liquidity 1, 3, 2, 5, 4,
         Convenience 1, 2, 3, 4, 5

**The Money Management IQ***

The student will be able to understand that:

*Primary Economic Understanding:* A spending and saving plan permits the family to think of alternative living plans and put in

---

Jack L. Taylor, Jr. and Arch W. Troelstrup, *The Consumer in American Society: Additional Dimensions* (New York: McGraw-Hill, 4th ed., 1970). Used with permission of McGraw-Hill Book Company.

# 106 Consumer Spending and Saving

priority personal goals and values.

*Secondary Economic Understanding:* A careful shopper considers many things such as quality, fashion changes, cost per unit, guarantees, time and energy.

*Purpose:* This questionnaire was selected to help the students understand their personal spending habits and evaluate them according to the accepted norms of money management.

*Materials and Instructions:* The Money Management IQ could be obtained from the listed book. Twenty questions are posed. Each correct answer is worth five points. A good, fair, and poor money management score is then determined for each student.

*Economic Content and Debriefing:* The test will show the students how they fare as money managers and will help them understand their weaknesses and strengths as consumers.

**The Monthly Cost Question:**

The student will be able to understand that:

*Primary Economic Understanding:* The cost of consumption before cash in hand is a large amount — about 18% interest. This compares to 15% of personal income usually spent on all clothing, personal and medical care.

*Secondary Economic Understanding:* The percent of time purchases relative to total income after tax should be controlled by the individual (15% of total income for time purchases is sometimes suggested as an appropriate ceiling).

*Purpose:* This activity will help students not only calculate interest charges on time purchases but relate those costs to overall personal income. This is the opportunity cost of consumption before cash-in-hand.

*Materials and Instructions:* Given a "salary," students will estimate deductions and take-home pay. Based on that income, students will choose an automobile and a house from newspaper ads and calculate the monthly bill for the automobile and the house.

*Procedure:*
Choose 10-15 different occupations and salaries (see Salary Chart below). List them on 3" x 5" cards. Randomly assign savings amounts. Distribute 1 card per student and have students calculate bi-weekly paycheck

Consumer Spending and Saving 107

deductions and take-home pay (See Deduction Chart below). Have them select an automobile to buy from ads and calculate financing, down payment and borrowing the rest for 4 years at 12%. Have them select a house from ads and calculate financing, putting 10-20-30% down and borrowing the rest for 30 years at 15%. Discuss budgets and have them plan how to spend the rest of their salary. Break into groups (of 2 or 3) of similar occupations and compare purchases with and budget. Ask students to defend their budget plans.

| OCCUPATIONS | SALARY BEFORE TAXES: |
|---|---|
| DOCTOR | $ 55,000 |
| LAWYER | 45,000 |
| C.P.A. | 30,000 |
| GROCERY STORE MANAGER | 15,000 |
| OFFICE CLERK | 12,000 |
| STORE CLERK | 8,000 |
| STEEL WORKER | $400/week* |
| SOCIAL SECURITY PENSION | $ 58/week |
| BANK CLERK | $150/week* |
| SCHOOL TEACHER | $275/week |
| LARGE CORPORATE EXECUTIVE | $200,000 |
| AUTO WORKER | $350/week* |
| PLUMBER | $ 15/hour |
| ORTHODONTIST | $ 80,000 |
| FARM OPERATOR | $156/week* |

Reprinted from "U.S. News & World Report," May 29, 1978, p. 77. Copyright 1978 U.S. News & World Report, Inc.

## DEDUCTIONS

| | | |
|---|---|---|
| SOCIAL SECURITY | 6% | 8% if self employed |
| FEDERAL WITHOLDING | 0% | less than 3,200 |
| | 10% | 3,200 - 12,000 |
| | 15% | 12,000 - 18,000 |
| | 20% | 18,000 - 25,000 |
| | 25% | 25,000 - 30,000 |
| | 30% | 30,000 - 40,000 |
| | 35% | 40,000 - 50,000 |
| | 40% | 50,000 - 60,000 |
| | 45% | 60,000 - 70,000 |
| | 50% | 70,000+ |
| CITY INCOME TAX | 1% | |
| STATE INCOME TAX | 2% | up to 25,000 |
| | 3% | 25,000+ |
| MEDICAL | $50-60/mo-single | You may determine |
| | $120/130/mo-married | what part business pays. |

### 108 Consumer Spending and Saving

*Economic Content and Debriefing:*

1. Credit consumption costs not only the purchase price of the good but substantial interest which means giving up (opportunity cost) other kinds of consumption.

2. The amount of monthly interest payments on time purchases should be considered as a percent of total monthly after-tax income.

3. The purchase of a home is personal investment which provides the family with a kind of savings.

4. The purchase of a home may be a hedge against inflation.

5. Federal Income tax is a progressive tax based on the concept of ability to pay.

6. As personal income rises a family may or may not spend a declining percent of its income for interest; that is, relatively reduce its time-purchases.

## Secondary Level Instruction

### Consumer Goals/Opportunity Cost:

The students will be able to understand that:

> *Primary Economic Understanding:* The principle of opportunity cost is important in analyzing buying problems.
>
> *Secondary Economic Understanding:* A spending plan permits a family to develop personal priority goals and values.

*Purpose:* The activity introduces the student to the opportunity cost concept in consumer decision-making; and identifies the need for individual consumers and families to establish personal short-run and long-run consumption goals.

*Materials and Instructions:*

1. All students will participate in a discussion of the following:
   a. consumer decision
   b. opportunity cost
   c. short-term goal
   d. long-term goal

2. Students will list on the chalkboard items of consumer importance, their price, possible opportunity costs and indicate whether they are short-term or long-term goals.

3. Each student will be given the "Consumer Decision Chart" below. In Column A the students are to indicate three consumer items of importance to them personally that could be considered short-term goals. They should also include the approximate cost of each item. In Column B, students are to list three opportunity costs for each of the items included in Column A.

4. Students will choose one item from Column A of their individual "Consumer Decision Chart" as a realistic short-term personal goal.

5. Students will explain, in paragraph form, the reasons underlying their individual consumer decisions. Such factors as personal income and need should be considered.

**CONSUMER DECISION CHART**

|  | A<br>If I buy: |  |  | B<br>Then I cannot buy: |
|---|---|---|---|---|
| 1. | _____ | Cost _____ | = | 1. _____<br>2. _____<br>3. _____ |
| 2. | _____ | Cost _____ | = | 1. _____<br>2. _____<br>3. _____ |
| 3. | _____ | Cost _____ | = | 1. _____<br>2. _____<br>3. _____ |

*Economic Content and Debriefing:*

1. When a consumer decision is made to purchase one item, the opportunity to purchase some other item is forgone (opportunity cost).

2. A good consumer buying plan should be both short-run and long-run.

3. Buying patterns or habits are influenced by many things such as: advertising, income, age, sex, education, peer pressures, climate, etc.

## Consumer Spending and Saving

**Hidden Costs:**

The student will be able to understand that:

> *Primary Economic Understanding:* The total costs of owning goods is the sum of the implicit (opportunity) costs and the explicit (out-of-pocket) costs.
>
> *Secondary Economic Understanding:* The implicit costs are the opportunity costs, in other words, the opportunity to invest the money and earn an income.
>
> The implicit cost can be calculated by the value of the good x the interest rate.

*Purpose:* To become aware of the total cost of a purchase by including implicit or hidden costs.

*Materials and Instructions:*

1. Select an item such as a washer that you plan to purchase. Find the total of the explicit costs including delivery, installation, etc.
2. Assume an alternative use for that amount of money such as investing it or depositing it in a savings account. Multiply the value of the washer x the interest rate. Add the implicit and explicit costs to find the total costs.

*Economic Content and Debriefing:*

1. The implicit costs are the opportunities that the individual gave up to use the money to buy a washer. That money may have been invested or deposited in a bank to earn interest.

2. The decision to buy the washer is one of several alternatives. Any alternative would give utility; this utility is foregone. If the money were deposited, interest income would have been earned; therefore, loss of interest income constitutes a hidden cost.

## Elementary Level Instruction

**Comparative Shopping:**

The student will be able to understand that:

> *Primary Economic Understanding:* A careful shopper considers many things such as quality, cost per unit, guarantees, and time and energy.

*Secondary Economic Understanding:* The time spent in Comparative Shopping should be included as part of the cost of shopping.

*Purpose:* This activity was developed in order to show the student that comparative shopping could result in savings for the household.

*Materials and Instructions:*

1. Have the students collect different grocery supermarket advertisements for similar items.
2. Develop a work sheet that will help the students analyze the advertisements. A work sheet could be developed for each store. The following are some sample questions that could be included in the worksheet:

    a. How many lemons could you buy for 80¢?
    b. If you buy both the Dynamo Liquid and the Lysol Cleaner, how much money do you save?
    c. Could you buy two pounds of brussel sprouts for $1.20?
    d. How many Tetley Tea bags do you get for 80¢?
    e. How much would a gallon of milk cost?

3. Develop another worksheet that will help students compare products and stores. The following are some sample questions that could be included in the worksheet:

    a. Would you rather buy your apples at store 1 or store 2? What is the difference in price?
    b. Where is the cheapest place to buy bacon? How much does it cost?
    c. Sugardale Coneys and Ball Park Franks are both hot dogs. Which cost more per pound? How much more?
    d. At which store would your groceries cost less?

*Economic Content and Debriefing:*

1. Comparative shopping does save the members of the family money which allows them to increase their standard of living.

2. The time used in comparative shopping should be viewed as a cost and be subtracted from the total savings in order to arrive at the actual real savings of comparative shopping. This is an expansion of the concept of opportunity cost. This assumes, however, that there is an alternative use for the time which has value.

## 112  Consumer Spending and Saving

**The Potato Chip Game:**

The student will be able to understand that:

*Primary Economic Understanding:* Advertising does influence the purchasing habits of household.

*Secondary Economic Understanding:* A careful shopper considers many things, such as cost per unit, quality and non-brandname merchandise.

*Purpose:* This simulation was developed to show the student that individual tastes differ and are influenced by advertising.

*Materials and Instructions:*

1. Purchase three brands of potato chips making sure that at least one of them is a nationally known brand.
2. Remove the potato chips from their original bags and place them in similar shopping bags labeled "A", "B", and "C".
3. Have the students taste, feel, etc. . . the different chips marked "A", "B", and "C".
4. Ask the students to indicate their preferences or votes for the different brands and calculate the results.
5. List the brand names in a different order on the chalkboard and have students individually indicate their preferences. The results should be listed on the chalkboard.
6. The results should then be matched and compared.

| Brand | Taste Preference | Brand Preference | Price |
|---|---|---|---|
| A | | | |
| B | | | |
| C | | | |

*Economic Content and Debriefing:*

1. In most cases the voting results will be different between the anonymous brands and the brand names.

2. A comparison of prices could be made to show how the smart shopper could reduce cost per unit.

3. Advertising does influence tastes as will be shown in the name recognition of the nationally advertised brand. What other role does advertising play?

# EVALUATION OF CONCEPT AREA V

1. How can a financial plan of spending and saving help a family define or clarify personal goals and values?

2. Define three characteristics of a good shopper.

3. How would you proceed to set up a family budget?

4. How does the principle of opportunity cost apply to consumer buying or budgeting problems?

5. As an individual why would you save?

6. Compare the advantages and disadvantages of three ways people hold savings.

7. Discuss three factors that should be considered by the individual before making a personal investment.

8. Discuss the characteristics of general investment opportunities available to Americans.

9. Describe a good personal investment plan.

10. Describe three types of insurance. How does insurance differ from personal investment?

11. Explain the considerations usually made in granting credit.

12. Evaluate three forms and costs of credit. When is the use of each form appropriate?

For reference, use List of Economic Understandings for this Concept Area.

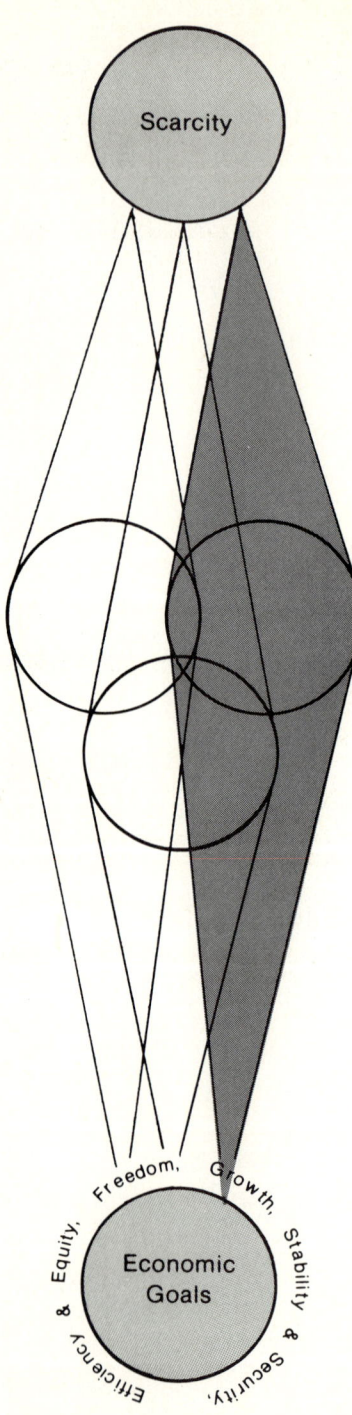

● -Director of Public Production (Spending and saving programs—as a citizen in one's democratic role.)

Complete code of screenings for Model on Page 6.

# THE ECONOMIC FUNCTIONS OF GOVERNMENT: FISCAL POLICY

## Concept Area VI

## Contents

**OVERVIEW OF CONCEPT AREA VI**     118

    Gross National Product    118
    Gross National Product Limitations    119
    Economic Functions of Government    119
    Fiscal Policy: Government Spending and Taxing    121
    Multiplier Effect    121

**LIST OF ECONOMIC UNDERSTANDINGS IN CONCEPT AREA VI**     122

**TEACHING APPLICATIONS IN CONCEPT AREA VI**     123

    **University Level Instruction**    123

       **Practice with Concept**    123
          1. Budget    123
          2. Multiplier    124
          3. Government Regulation Agencies    125

    **Secondary Level Instruction**    128

          1. Clarify Reagan Tax Cuts Through 1984 Newspaper Clipping    128
          2. Government Expenditures    130

    **Elementary Level Instruction**    132

          1. Who Pays for the Schools?    132
          2. Let's Have a Party    133

**EVALUATION INSTRUMENT OF CONCEPT AREA VI**     135

## OVERVIEW OF CONCEPT AREA VI

**GROSS NATIONAL PRODUCT.** To measure the impact of government on the United States economy, a measuring device of economic activity for the whole economy is needed. The popular measurement among economists is *Gross National Product* (GNP) which is defined as the market value of all final goods and services produced in a country over a period of one year. The most direct way of calculating GNP (the market value of final goods and services) is to look at all spending agents (sectors) in the economy (households, government, business and foreigners) and calculate how much they spend in a given year. This is referred to as the expenditure approach to calculating GNP. Often this aggregate economic activity is stated as GNP = C + I + G + X - M where,

- C = household consumption expenditure on both domestic and foreign products,
- I = business investment expenditures on capital goods and changes in inventories + private household residential construction.
- G = government (federal, state and local) expenditures on goods and services.
- X - M = net exports; exports less imports are already included in consumption (C) and need to be deducted.

In order to compare GNP from one year to the next, real GNP must be determined because market values (prices) of goods and services change at different rates during different years. Real GNP is GNP adjusted for inflation in terms of a base year. Converting the adjusted or real GNP to a per capita basis (by dividing real GNP by population) and then examining how fast this per capita figure is growing gives an idea of how much individual welfare or the standard of living is rising.

In 1976 government expenditures on goods and services amounted to approximately 365.5 billion dollars out of a GNP of 1,691.6 billion dollars at 1976 prices. This amounts to approximately 21.5% of total expenditures on final goods and services in the United States in 1976. This, however, is an underestimation of government presence, as approximately 191.3 billion dollars spent by households as part of consumption expenditures, originates in the government budget and finds its way to household expenditures in the form of transfer payments. Transfer payments are payments made by the government without receiving a good or service in exchange. Such payments include as unemployment compensation, aid to dependent children (welfare), medicaid, etc. Combining government expenditures with transfer payments shows the government budget to be in control of approximately 32.9% of expenditures on goods and services in the 1976 economy.

**GROSS NATIONAL PRODUCT LIMITATIONS.** While GNP is the best measure we have to summarize the overall level of market activity of the economy, there are weaknesses in the measure. For example, *GNP does not reflect the purpose of production. It does not include most goods and services that are not for sale,* such as the labor of women maintaining their households and *it does not consider the value of leisure.* Further, to assume the "welfare" of the country is in direct relationship to the level of real GNP may be in error. If in one year GNP rises by a billion dollars, owing to an increase in expenditures in education and the next year it rises by the same amount because of a rise in tobacco production, the figures in both years show the same amount of "growth" of GNP. The problem of environmental deterioration complicates the measure further. Some types of GNP growth directly contribute to pollution—automobile and paper for example. As a result economists treat GNP in a reserved manner insofar as "welfare" is concerned. Paul Samuelson suggests a new measure Net Economic Welfare—to supplement GNP. Tobin and Norhaus propose a MEW—Measure of Economic Welfare—which would subtract the output that contributes nothing to the sum of individuals' utilities and add in other sums which contribute to human welfare. While the appearance of such new measures may increase, the practical aspects of perfecting such measures would appear to obviate rapid adoption of these measures for analytical purposes.

**ECONOMIC FUNCTIONS OF GOVERNMENT.** Economists have traditionally classified the economic presence of government in the economy into four main functions, namely *allocation of resources, regulation of business and markets, redistribution of income and the promotion of stability and growth in the economy.* These are exclusively economic functions that are added to the political, social and legal functions of government. Some functions delegated to government by the society come from a partial failure of the market sector to adequately perform those functions according to the standards set by our democratically elected government.

First, government (at all levels) influences the *allocation of resources* in the economy by producing public goods that, due to their characteristics, could not be produced by the market sector. These are goods and services that, if provided to one individual, are provided to all individuals in equal amounts. Thus, it is very hard to exclude anyone from their consumption, e.g., national defense and fire and police protection. In order to provide these services, their producer has to have the power to coerce people to pay for the public good and thus the power to tax. Another kind of service, where government influences the amount of resources allocated to its production, is merit goods. These are provided by the market sector but in relatively smaller amounts than the political process deems necessary, e.g., educational services and health services. The government feels obligated to add to the market supply of these goods and services. Citizens have some control over how much public and merit goods are provided by electing congressmen and by participating in the Congressional budgetary hearings through their elected representatives. Money collected by government as taxes is money not available to the individual for spending nor to the private sector for business expansion and job creation.

Second, the government *regulates some of the market sectors' output* and allocation of resources in order to promote competition when this is absent, and to protect the health of the general public whether as consumers or workers. Anti-trust laws were established in order to prevent market domination by one or several producers since such domination usually results in higher prices for the consumer. Other forms of regulation exist in terms of specialized government agencies that monitor and correct a particular market or function in the economy, e.g., the Securities and Exchange Commision and the Occupational Safety and Health Agency. There is an ongoing debate in the United States regarding the degree of government regulation in the economy since the regulation of business usually results in regulation or reduction of the individual choices.

Third, the government actively participates in *redistributing income* among the various segments of the population. Through the tax and transfer payment system the government is able to promote a relatively more equal distribution of income after taxes and transfer payments than before. This is basically done by setting different income standards that qualify households to either pay taxes, or, collect benefits that will somewhat reduce the severity of their poverty. The government's tax revenues are generated by many kinds of taxes and it is impossible to determine which tax dollar performs which specific function. The government also conducts, consciously or unconsciously, many income redistribution programs by returning to certain geographical areas more funds than they had contributed to the federal treasury, thus transferring resources from the wealthier more industrialized regions to the poorer less industrialized ones.

Finally, the government, following the passage of the Employment Act of 1946, has actively attempted *to stabilize the economy and promote economic growth* primarily by means of fiscal policy. This function of government developed because real GNP traditionally has increased over time in a cyclical fashion. This behavior is called the business cycle in economic literature. Study of the business cycle shows that expenditures fluctuate over time resulting in periods of recession (when actual expenditures decline below the desired level that will generate full employment in the economy) and periods of inflation (when actual expenditures exceed the desired level necessary to generate full employment in the economy).

**FISCAL POLICY: GOVERNMENT SPENDING AND TAXING.** The government (mostly at the federal level) has initiated two kinds of programs to stabilize the economy, i.e., eliminate the fluctuation in real GNP, and induce it to grow at a desired rate that will provide both full employment and stable prices. First, *discretionary fiscal policy* which results in the government increasing or reducing its expenditures and/or taxes depending on the behavior of the other spending units in the economy, namely, households (C) or businesses (I). This is a very complicated process that involves many problems, such as estimating accurately future expenditures by households and business and the time lag between the time the political process makes a fiscal decision and the actual implementation of it. Second, *automatic fiscal policy* which does not require any conscious action on the part of the government but rather is initiated automatically when real GNP declines. An example would be when a layoff occurs unemployment compensation increases household income: thus family expenditures do not decline as much as they otherwise would. Fiscal policies for government spending and taxation have been intiated by the government to stabilize the economy and promote growth. They may be discretionary or automatic. Fiscal Policy and Monetary Policy (Concept VII) are the primary techniques the federal government uses to stabilize the economy. The ability of the government to use monetary and fiscal tools to "even out" the business cycle does not mean, however, that these tools make it possible to carefully control the economy. This is not the case.

**MULTIPLIER EFFECT.** If the government wishes to increase GNP by a certain amount, it does not necessarily have to increase its expenditures or reduce taxes by the whole amount of the desired increase. This results from the fact that every dollar spent by the government, business and the consumer is income for someone else who will also save a portion of it and spend the rest. Therefore each additional expenditure results in a second expenditure and a larger increase in GNP than the original dollar amount spent. The extent of the increase in GNP will depend on the portion of each income dollar not spent. The smaller the amount not spent (saved or taxed away) the larger the increase in GNP. This concept is called the *multiplier effect* and results in further complications in fiscal policy decision making.

The debate of precisely what the role of the government should be, has been and continues to be, one of the primary concerns of all Americans.

# LIST OF ECONOMIC UNDERSTANDINGS IN CONCEPT AREA VI

1. Gross national product (GNP) measures the market value of all final goods and services produced in a country over a period of one year.

2. Real GNP measures the value of output in the economy of a particular year at a base year's prices. Adjusting these prices to base year prices allows comparisons of data for different years.

3. In 1976 the government budget accounted for approximately 33% of GNP in the U.S.

4. Transfer payments are payments made by the government without the production of a good or service in exchange.

5. The government allocates resources through producing public goods and merit goods.

6. The government promotes competition and protects the economic welfare of workers and consumers.

7. The government redistributes income among individuals and groups.

8. The goal of the government is to stabilize and promote growth in the economy through the use of fiscal policy; policies of government relevant to spending and taxing.

9. Discretionary fiscal policy is the deliberate manipulation of the federal budget to increase or decrease public or private expenditure in order to influence real GNP.

10. Automatic fiscal policy is the automatic response of government budget to changes in private spending.

# TEACHING APPLICATIONS IN CONCEPT AREA VI

## University Level Instruction

**Practice With Concept:**

- In 1976, the federal government budget accounted for 33% of the total GNP. What percentage does the federal budget account for today? To what do you attribute the difference? What advantages and disadvantages are there to increased/decreased government spending?
- Identify public and merit goods provided in your community. Does the private sector also provide for some of these goods? Explain the difference between similar goods provided by government and provided by the private sector.
- Collect newspaper and news magazine articles which explain current fiscal policy actions. What outcomes are aimed for with particular fiscal measures?
- Explain how the government regulates actions of businesses in your community. What is the purpose of such regulation? What are the effects of regulation?

**Budget***

The students will understand that:

> *Primary Economic Understanding:* The government sector in the U.S. accounts for approximately one third of GNP.
>
> *Secondary Economic Understanding:* The determination of the Federal Government Budget is a very complex matter that involves compromises on the part of the various special interest groups involved in the budgetary process.
>
> *Purpose:* This simulation introduces the student to the complex federal budgetary process.

---

*\*Budget: A simulation of the struggle for money in the national budgeting process* by Charles L. Kennedy, Interact Company, Post Office Box 262, Lakeside, California 92040, 1973.

*Materials and Instructions:* This is a commercially produced game that can be purchased from the publisher. It is a rather complicated simulation which involves all the participants in determining the composition of a hypothetical budget for the federal government. Students are given individual ID cards describing the roles they are to assume. They are also given individual goal cards . . . . each would like to see . . . . The I.D.'s will be known to all participants. This will help in determining the various opponents and proponents of the various items within the budget. The role assignments guarantee that individual participants will pursue their own interest rather than attempt to influence the whole budget. Each student is also assigned a particular number of votes in the House of Representatives and the Senate. Votes are cast after the budget has been approved by the Appropriations Committees and has reached the floor of both houses. Therefore, the students will discover that they have to be aware of the strengths and weaknesses involved of all the positions.

*Economic Content and Debriefing:*

1. Determination of the budget is a very involved process that is based on compromise between the various special interest groups participating in the process.

2. The various government departments and functions are constantly bargaining, through their supporters, for larger allocations within the budget.

3. The two positions that usually emerge from the bargaining process is a pro-defense group and an anti-defense group. Other differences also develop that usually hold the ultimate balance of power.

4. The budgetary process involves many steps. It starts at the Executive branch and passes through the Senate and House of Representatives Appropriations Committees. Students should be able to see that they can influence the budget at any one of these terminals and should they fail at one point they may try the others.

5. The final budget is a compromise between the various groups formulating the budget. No one group achieves all its goals.

**Multiplier***

The student will be able to understand that:

*Primary Economic Understanding:* The multiplier principle states

---

*\*Multiplier* by Tuckman, B., & Tuckman, H. Toward a more effective economic principles class. *The Journal of Economic Education,* 1976, Special Issue *3,* 3-72.

that an increase in expenditures by the government, or any other sector in the economy, will result in a larger increase in GNP than the initial increase.

*Secondary Economic Understanding:* The larger the leakage from each expenditure into savings, taxes and imports the smaller will be the size of the multiplier.

*Purpose:* This activity shows the student the importance of recognizing the multiplier effect in making fiscal policy decisions. It could also be used to demonstrate the relationship between the size of the multiplier and leakage from the spending stream.

*Materials and Instructions:*

1. Photocopy one side of a dollar bill.
2. Divide the bill into one hundred equal squares and number them.
3. Pass the dollar bill among the students. Each student clips out the number of cents that he/she would save out of the dollar if they had earned it, and then passes the remaining portion to the next person.
4. Have students record the number of cents that he or she has spent.
5. By adding all expenditures the class will be able to arrive at the impact of that dollar spent on GNP.

*Economic Content and Debriefing:*

1. People have different propensities to spend and save.

2. If the leakage is increased to include imports and taxes, the final effect on total expenditures would be smaller, i.e., the multiplier would be smaller.

**Government Regulation Agencies***

The student will be able to understand that:

*Primary Economic Understanding:* The government promotes competition and protects the economic welfare of consumers and workers.

*Secondary Economic Understanding:* Government regulation is a very complex matter that utilizes a large amount of scarce resources.

---

*The Grand Scale of Federal Intervention* Reprinted from the April 4, 1977 issue of Business Week by special permission, (c) 1977 by McGraw-Hill, Inc., New York, NY 10020. All rights reserved.

*Purpose:* This exercise was developed to show the student examples of government regulation of the economy. It is meant to direct the students to form their own opinions on the extent of government regulation of the system.

*Materials and Instructions:*

1. Reproduce the examples found on pp. 114-115 or refer to the more complete 27-agency description given in April 4, 1977, pp. 52-56, *Business Week*.
2. Have the students review the agencies and discuss the contents.

*Economic Content and Debriefing:*

1. Government regulation is a very complex process that involves many different agencies on different levels.

2. Government agencies may develop from market failure to perform a particular function.

3. Government regulation involves costs and benefits. Research effectiveness and efficiency of government regulations are important to the society.

## THE GRAND SCALE OF FEDERAL INTERVENTION

Hundreds of federal departments, agencies, divisions, and bureaus regulate to one degree or another the nation's commerce. Below are examples of the most powerful and pervasive of the U.S. government's economic and social regulators.

*Finance Example*

Agency: Securities and Exchange Commission
Vital Statistics: Created in 1934, it has 2,000 employees, 16 field offices, and a budget of $56 million.
Major Functions: Regulates all publicly traded securities and the markets on which they are traded. Administers public disclosure laws and polices security fraud.
Special Characteristics: Most prestigious of the independent agencies, the commission has a reputation—occasionally unmerited—for aggressive policework and zealous protection of investors. Current preoccupations: foreign bribes and creation of a national securities market.

*Competition Example*

Agency: Interstate Commerce Commission
Vital Statistics: Created in 1887, it has 2,100 employees, 79 field offices and a $57 million budget.
Major Functions: Regulates rates and routes of railroads, most truckers, and some waterway carriers.
Special Characteristics: The oldest and most hidebound independent regulator, it spends most of its time adjudicating motor-carrier tariffs and operating rights, is deeply committed to keeping competition among carriers in delicate balance.

*Employment Example*

Agency: Equal Employment Opportunity Commission
Vital Statistics: Created in 1964, it employs 2,500, maintains 39 field offices, and will spend $70 million this year.
Major Functions: Investigates and conciliates complaints of employment discrimination based on race, religion, and sex.
Special Characteristics: Although it has filed—and won—some big court cases involving millions of dollars in back-pay awards, the commission is essentially without powers or real authority. It may be folded into a unified anti-discriminating agency.

*Employment Example*

Agency: National Labor Relations Board
Vital Statistics: Created in 1935, the board has 2,700 employees in Washington and in 48 field offices, and a budget of $83 million.
Major Functions: Regulates labor practices of unions and companies and conducts representation elections.
Special Characteristics: Basically a judicial agency, the board conciliates or decides thousands of cases brought each year by individuals, unions, and companies complaining of unfair or illegal labor practices. The board is considered one of the slowest agencies in Washington.

*Energy Example*

Agency: Federal Energy Administration
Vital Statistics: Launched in 1973, it has 4,000 employees, nine field

offices, and a budget this fiscal year of $156 million. Administers $840 million for strategic petroleum storage.

Major Functions: Controls price of most domestic crude oil and some refined products, principally gasoline. Charged with developing a national energy policy.

Special Characteristics: Created in the crisis of the Arab oil embargo, it has been anything but an enthusiastic regulator. The agency may disappear into a new Cabinet-level Energy Department.

*Safety Example*

Agency: National Highway Traffic Safety Administration

Vital Statistics: Created in 1970, it has 800 employees, 10 field offices, and a $100 million budget. It also administers $129 million in grants to states.

Major Functions: Regulates manufacturers of autos, trucks, buses, motorcycles, trailers, and tires in an effort to reduce the number and severity of traffic accidents.

Special Characteristics: An aggressive young regulator, it has promulgated hundreds of regulations on everything from auto bumpers to mandatory seat belt installation. Its new administrator comes from Ralph Nader's organization.

## Secondary Level Instruction

### Clarify Reagan Tax Cuts Through 1984—Newspaper clipping*

The student will understand that:

*Primary Economic Understanding:* The government influences the allocation of resources in the economy by producing public and merit goods. To provide these services the government must have the power to tax.

*Secondary Economic Understanding:* Citizens have some control over how much public and merit goods are provided by participating in budget hearings and by directing their elected representatives.

---

*Clarify Reagan Tax Cuts Through 1984* Ashland Times-Gazette, June 6, 1981. Reprinted by permission of United Press International.

*Purpose:* Individuals, through the voting process and through their elected representatives, are responsible to control the amount of tax and therefore the amount of public and merit goods provided by the government.

*Materials and Instructions:* Select four to six students to conduct a group study. Have the group select a chairperson. Give each student in the group a copy of the news clipping (on next page) and the following instructions for conducting the study.

1. Review the article to
   a. Define the problem.
   b. Point out the conclusions or goals.
2. Identify the relevant economic principles or concepts.
3. Analyze the alternatives.
4. Choose and support your alternatives.
   a. Point out why you do or do not agree with conclusions of the article.

Allow between thirty and forty-five minutes for group study (overnight assignment is even better); then ask the group or a spokesperson for the group to report the conclusions of the group to the class and lead a discussion with the entire class.

*Economic Content and Debriefing:*

1. The portion of national income spent by government reduces the amount of discretionary personal income available for consumer goods and services. The opportunity cost in a society of increased government expenditures is reduced individual expenditures.

2. In the final analysis, through their elected representatives, individuals are responsible for the tax levels and redistribution of income. The appropriateness or "justice" of a given tax is viewed differently by different people.

3. There are negative as well as positive impacts of a rising tax level. The economic growth of a society may be jeopardized by a high tax level through reduced incentive to invest and to produce.

4. The tradeoff between economic equity, which is difficult to determine, and economic growth is an on-going debate in any society. The appropriateness or "justice" of a given tax is viewed differently by different people.

## ASHLAND TIMES-GAZETTE

131st YEAR — NUMBER 133    ASHLAND, OHIO 44805    SATURDAY EVENING, June 6, 1981

# Clarify Reagan tax cuts through 1984

WASHINGTON (UPI) — Under the administration's new tax cut proposal, a one-income family earning $25,000 would save more than $1,000 in taxes in 1984, but in 1981 the reduction would amount to only 1.25 percent.

The Treasury Department estimates a family with one wage earner and a $25,000 income would save $1,056 in 1984, when the administration's 33-month, 25 percent tax cut is fully effective.

A couple with two incomes totaling $25,000 would pay $1,441 less in taxes in 1984 than under existing tax rates, the department said.

The proposal, backed by a bipartisan group of lawmakers, includes several changes in the tax code, such as a reduction in the inheritance tax and the so-called "marriage penalty" and a new depreciation schedule for business investments.

But because the effective date of the individual tax cut would be Oct. 1, the first fiscal year's 5 percent cut would apply only to three months of the 1981 calendar year. Thus, the first-year rate reduction would be only 1.25 percent, Treasury Secretary Donald Regan said Friday.

The second and third fiscal years would each get 10 percent tax cuts, but on a calendar year basis withholding tables in 1982 would reflect tax cuts of between 5 and 10 percent.

The tax-writing House Ways and Means Committee plans to begin work on a tax cut bill next week, although its version probably will reflect the two-year, 15 percent outline agreed to by the panel's Democrats.

The White House said President Reagan's pledge to not campaign against Democrats who support his tax cut only applies to those who continue to support future administration policy decisions.

"As long as people are going to support him, he's not going to go out and campaign against them," said James Baker, the White House chief of staff. "If, on the other hand, they should turn on him — then the bet's off."

Some southern conservative Democrats had bargained to vote for Reagan's tax cut plan if the president would not campaign against their reelection. Baker said the president's affirmative agreement was not a "carte blanche" offer.

"What he said was, 'I will not campaign in your districts if you are supportive of my legislative program,'" said acting press secretary Larry Speakes. "If they voted against him on other programs, then the pledge would not hold .... They've got to be at least supportive of his programs as they go in the next 18 months."

The flurry of official comment spelling out the president's deal indicates Reagan is looking for a reliable coalition that could be formed on every issue.

"Obviously he would like to see a coalition, a reasonably permanent coalition, built here during the four years of his administration," said Baker.

## Government Expenditures

The student will understand that:

> *Primary Economic Understanding:* Government—Local, State and Federal—account for approximately 33% of GNP in the U.S.A.

## The Economic Functions of Government: Fiscal Policy

*Secondary Economic Understanding:* Government allocates resources through producing public goods and redistributes income among individuals by taxation and transfer payments.

*Purpose:* This activity introduces to the student two important functions of government—purchase of goods collectively for the welfare of the people and redistribution of income to alleviate poverty and suffering of some of its people.

*Materials and Instructions:*

1. List on the board the eleven expenditure categories that appear on the Government Expenditures Pie Chart below.
2. Ask students to divide the percent of expenditures they believe appropriate to each category. This should equal 100%.
3. Distribute to the students the following graphic presentation of Federal, State and Local Government Expenditures 1979. Ask students to calculate their percent of error for each entry.
4. The teacher should then lead a discussion as to the rationale of the distribution of government revenue as well as support and criticism of that distribution. Ask what percent is government spending of total GNP?

General Expenditures of Federal, State and Local Governments by Functions, 1978

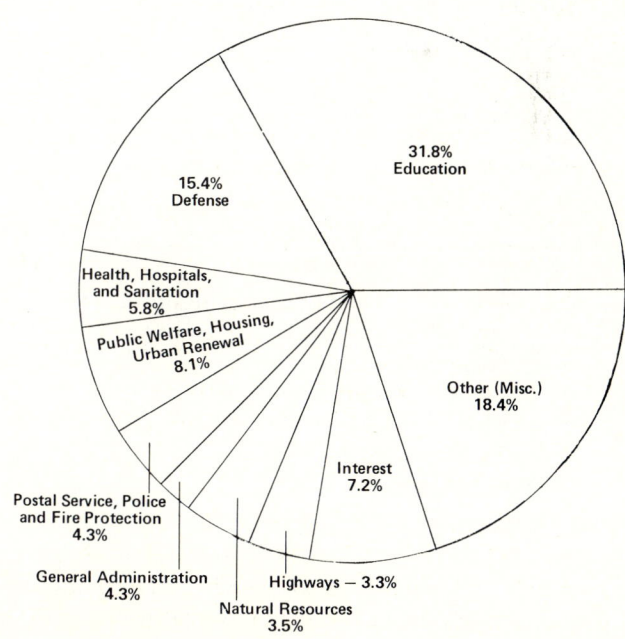

## 132 The Economic Functions of Government: Fiscal Policy

*Economic Content and Debriefing:*

1. Some economic goods are more appropriately provided by the public sector; e.g., defense.

2. As the share of national income spent by government increases, the share of national income spent by individuals falls.

3. Through the US tax and transfer payment system, the government redistributes income. This is basically done by setting different income standards that qualify households to either pay taxes or collect benefits.

4. Income redistribution by the government takes place not only among individuals but geographic regions as well.

## Elementary Level Instruction

**Who Pays for the Schools?**

The student will understand that:

> *Primary Economic Understanding:* There are three levels of government and they perform different activities.
> 
> *Secondary Economic Understanding:* Taxes are the main source of revenue for the government.
> 
> Each level of government collects different taxes to finance its activities.

*Purpose:* This activity demonstrates to the students that government spending is beneficial to society as a whole, however, it does impose a burden on the taxpayers.

*Materials and Instructions:*

1. Collect pictures from magazines of different activities performed by the different levels of government. For example for local government, pictures of schools, fire stations, police departments, community swimming pool, etc.; for state government, pictures of state parks, interstate highways, highway patrol, national guard, etc.; and for the federal government pictures of space exploration, national defense, national parks, U.S. embassies, etc. . . .
2. Have the students select different pictures, describe what they are, state the level of government that provides the service and the kinds of taxes used to finance them.

*Economic Content and Debriefing:*

1. Each different level of government performs different functions.
2. Taxes collected are used to provide government services.
3. The main sources of revenue for the federal government are personal income taxes, corporation income tax, social security taxes and gift and estate taxes.
4. The main source of revenue for most state governments is the sales tax and the state income tax.
5. The main sources of revenue for local governments are property taxes and city income taxes.

**Let's Have A Party**

The student will understand that:

> *Primary Economic Understanding:* Governments at all levels provide services for their citizens in exchange for the tax revenues they receive from their citizens.
>
> *Secondary Economic Understanding:* Taxes are a necessary and positive contribution to government's operation.
>
> Taxes are levied in different ways and in varying amounts to different groups of people, i.e. real estate taxes to home owners, sales taxes to home owners, sales taxes to consumers, corporate taxes to corporations, road use taxes to semi truck owners. Each tax is determined differently.
>
> Groups which contribute more heavily in the taxation process may make the greatest claims for services in return.

*Purpose:* This activity was designed to create a balance in understanding students have towards taxes. Through its simple procedure, students will be aware of the positive value taxation can have in our society.

*Materials and Instructions:*
1. There are no special materials needed for this activity, unless the teacher wishes to pictorially demonstrate the variety of services government performs following taxation.
2. Finding an excuse to reward the students, acts as the stimulus for this activity, i.e., they have been exceptionally accurate on their latest homework exercises. The class on the average scored well on their last test, etc.

## 134  The Economic Functions of Government: Fiscal Policy

3. Once the students have been sufficiently complimented on their latest achievement, state you wish to reward them by giving them a party of *their* choice. You volunteer to pay for and provide *EVERYTHING* for their party, and they may have the party *ANYWHERE* they would like. It is important that the class be given some freedom to develop its excitement and mentally calculate all the wants for their *"NO HOLDS BARRED"* Party.

4. Usually a student will pick up on the idea of a 'no-free lunch' concept and question "what's the catch?" or, if no one does question your generosity casually mention there is however, *ONE* requirement for the party... *DON'T INVITE ANY FORM OF GOVERNMENT!!!!*

5. Since government is often thought of as a uniform the subtlety of government may go unnoticed until detail planning for the party begins.

6. Allow the students to discuss amoung themselves what, where, when, etc. they want for the party (reminding them *NOT* to include government), quickly, the question of *what* to have at the party will be eliminated because *MONEY* can not be used to buy anything. The party can't take place *anywhere* because of property taxes, real estate, local school millage, etc. on the land owner. *When* to have the pary is also a time function which is regulated by government (E.S.T., M.S.T., P.S.T.). Many services performed or provided by government may demonstrated, such as food for the party comes under federal, state and local food regulations for quality control and health protection (Jungle, Sinclair Lewis).

7. Challenge the class to see how many government functions can be listed on the board. At the conclusion, point out that these vital services are possible because the general welfare is sustained through a taxation system.

*Economic Content and Debriefing:*

1. Levels of government taxation vary for different purposes and different population groups.

2. Taxes levied on various commodities or services may be held to revert back to the facilitation of that good or service area, i.e. road-use taxes or gasoline taxes may go for the repairing of highways.

3. Government functions for the general welfare of the people and therefore the costs of government must be derived from the population.

4. Benefits derived from government due to taxation may not always be visible, i.e. strategic air command, vital missiles, etc.

# EVALUATION OF CONCEPT AREA VI

1. Describe two methods of calculating the GNP.

2. Identify the entries in GNP = C + I + G + X - M.

3. Explain how the GNP or the level of economic activity of one year may be adjusted to compare it to another year.

4. Governmental expenditures in 1976 were what percent of total US expenditures?

5. Discuss the purpose and character of two transfer payments of the Federal Government.

6. At what point do you believe the increase of Federal Government spending should be stopped? Why?

7. Evaluate three economic roles of the Federal Government.

8. How does the Federal Government attempt to promote competition among business? Why?

9. Evaluate the purposes for which the Federal Government redistributes income.

10. What was the goal of the Employment Act of 1946?

11. Compare discretionary fiscal policy with automatic fiscal policy.

12. Explain the multiplier effect.

13. What are the major sources of revenue and major expenditures for the federal government?

14. How effective is the Federal Government in reducing the fluctuations of the business cycle with the use of fiscal policy?

For reference, use List of Economic Understandings for this Concept Area.

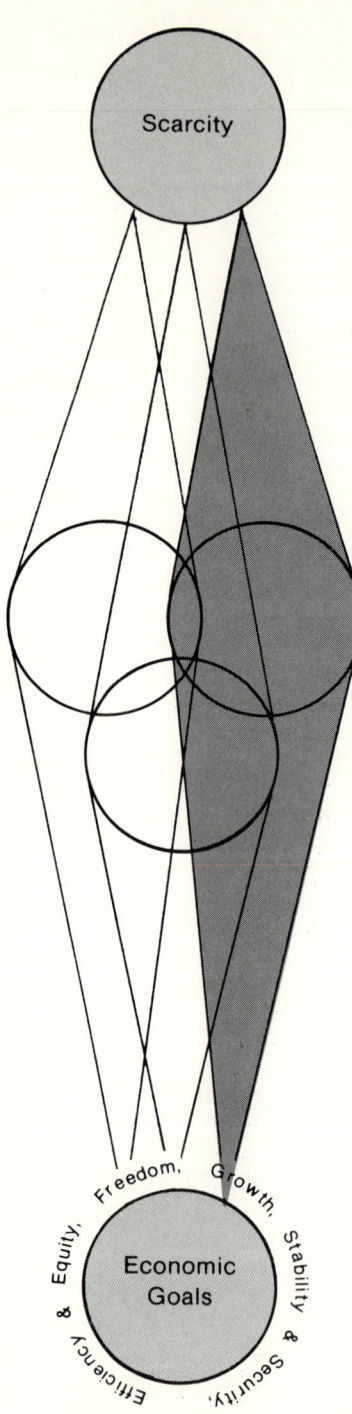

— Director of Public Production (Spending and saving programs—as a citizen in one's democratic role.)

Complete code of screenings for Model on Page 6.

# MONEY, MONETARY POLICY AND THE FEDERAL RESERVE SYSTEM

## Concept Area VII

## Contents

**OVERVIEW OF CONCEPT AREA VII**     138

   Forms of Money    138
   Quantity Equation of Exchange    138
   The Federal Reserve System and Monetary Policy    139
   Money Supply    140
   Multiple Banks Credit Expansion    140
   Impact of Monetary Policy on Inflation and Unemployment    141

**LIST OF ECONOMIC UNDERSTANDINGS IN CONCEPT AREA VII**     142

**TEACHING APPLICATIONS IN CONCEPT AREA VII**     143

   **University Level Instruction**    143

      Practice with Concept    143
         1. Tight Rope    143
         2. How to Cure Inflation    144
         3. Chase Cuts Prime to 20% From 20½% Newspaper Clipping    145

   **Secondary Level Instruction**    148

         1. The Federal Reserve System    148
         2. You're a Banker    150

   **Elementary Level Instruction**    151

         1. How would You Pay?    151
         2. Trade-offs, Lesson 9 ("Why Money?")    152

**EVALUATION INSTRUMENT OF CONCEPT AREA VII**     154

## OVERVIEW OF CONCEPT AREA VII

**FORMS OF MONEY.** Money is the most liquid asset that an individual or firm can own. It is accepted in exchange for most goods and services available on the market. Therefore, one can expect that money plays an important role in any economy. This observation was recognized very early in history and has been accepted since.

In the American economic system approximately 75% of the total supply of money is in the form of *checking accounts* (demand deposits) and *not in coins and bills*. American money is not backed by any precious metal, but it derives its value from government decree, the strength of the American economy and its general acceptance as a medium of exchange. Money also fulfills the function of a storehouse and measure of value.

**QUANTITY EQUATION OF EXCHANGE.** The amount of money available in an economy is very important for the economic health of a society because it affects that society's level of spending. The level of spending determines the amount of goods and services produced in the economy which in turn determines real income, employment and prices all of which are important barometers of economic health. The level of spending is also affected by how quickly households and firms spend the money that they have (this turnover rate of money is referred to as velocity of circulation). Thus an increase or decrease in total spending may be related to an increase or decrease in the supply of money, in the velocity of circulation, or both. This relationship can be seen directly from the *quantity equation of exchange* which is customarily written as $MV = PQ$ where M is the stock of money in the economy at a particular time; V is the velocity of circulation, or the average number of times that each dollar is spent during the year; P is the price of each commodity that enters into the national income for the year; and Q is the quantity of each commodity that enters into national income or product that year.

One explanation of the equation is that every sales transaction amounts to the price of the unit (P) times the quantity sold (Q). This product (PQ) equals the total national income or product for the economy that year. The units are paid for by (MV), the stock of money times its velocity of circulation, which also equals the national income or product for the year. We can see that if the velocity of circulation (V) remained stable in an economy over a period of time and the money supply increased, then (PQ) will have to increase in response. This increase can take place in the quantity of goods and services produced (Q) in the prices of goods and services (P) or in some combination of the two. Which variable will increase will depend on how close the economy is to its full production capacity. If all resources are tied up in production, an increase in the money supply (M) will be reflected usually as an increase in prices (P), i.e. inflation. If there are idle resources that could be used to produce goods and services, an increase in the money supply usually will result in an increase in the quantity of goods and services produced (Q). This is a desirable effect as it increases society's real income whereas an increase in prices only increases society's nominal or money income which does not increase the standard of living. Thus it could be stated that since spending is crucial to the level of income; and spending is done with money, money and the factors affecting its supply are crucial to the determination of the level of economic activity.

**FEDERAL RESERVE SYSTEM AND MONETARY POLICY.** The function of regulating the money supply is usually delegated by the government to a central bank which supervises most of the financial functions in the economy. In the United States this function is performed by the *Federal Reserve System* which was established in 1913. The Fed, as it is called, consists of twelve federal reserve banks and is controlled by the Board of Governors, a group of seven members appointed by the President of the United States. All national banks (commercial banks chartered by the federal governments), and some state banks (chartered by state governments), belong to the Federal Reserve system. They are referred to as member banks. The Fed, through controlling the member banks, is able to control the money supply, i.e. conduct its *monetary policy,* to promote economic stability and growth. The Fed has the following primary tools at its disposal to administer monetary policy:

- Open market operations: the sale or purchase of government securities between the Fed's holdings and the general public.
- Legal required reserves of member banks: changing the percentage of demand deposits that a member bank must keep in cash or as deposits with the federal reserve bank.
- The discount rate: changing the rate of interest federal reserve banks charge on loans to member banks.

Once the Fed has determined the kind of monetary policy needed it proceeds to use these three tools to adjust the money supply to reflect these policies. If the decision is to reduce the money supply (tight monetary policy) the Fed could sell government securities on the open market, raise the discount rate or raise the legal reserve requirements. If the decision is to increase the money supply (easy monetary policy) the Fed could buy government securities on the open market, reduce the discount rate or reduce the legal reserve requirements. Actually, monetary policy is conducted through open market operations only, with the legal reserve requirements and the discount rate adjusted periodically to reflect the general monetary conditions rather than initiate policy.

The three tools of monetary policy work through their impact on member banks' excess reserves, i.e. the reserves that banks have available to loan. The amount of excess reserves that bankers hold determines the monetary climate of the economy. If they hold large amounts of excess reserves then they are more ready to make loans and charge relatively low interest rates. If they hold a small amount of excess reserves then credit conditions will be tight and the interest rates charged will be relatively high. Member banks' excess reserves are determined by their total reserves (cash holdings and deposits with a federal reserve bank) less the legal required reserves (that portion of total reserves that is required in cash or deposits with a federal reserve bank).

**MONEY SUPPLY.** Thus, each of the tools of monetary policy can affect the *level of excess reserves* held by member banks. In the case of open market operations the sale of government securities by the Fed to the public involves the exchange of these government bonds for a check written on the U.S.A's account with a member bank. The Fed then reduces the deposits of that member bank by the amount of the check, which in turn reduces the member bank's total reserves by the same amount. Therefore, the bank's excess reserves will be reduced to reflect this drop in total reserves. The opposite effect takes place when the Fed purchases a government bond from the public, thus increasing the member banks' excess reserves. The bank is then able to use a portion of these reserves to make loans to individuals and to businesses. These loaned or created monies serve to increase the money supply.

In the case of a reduction in legal required reserves, excess reserves directly increase even though total reserves remain unchanged because reserves that were tied up in legal required reserves are now free and available for lending, as excess reserves. A reduction in the discount rate allows member banks to borrow reserves from the Fed at a relatively lower cost which in turn increases their total reserves and consequently their excess reserves by the same amount.

**MULTIPLE BANKS CREDIT EXPANSION.** The banking system as a whole can *create money* (in the form of checking accounts), because one bank's loans are another bank's deposits. The extent of this process of credit expansion available to the banking system as a whole depends on the percent of deposits that must be held as legal required reserves. For example, assume the reserve requirement is 20% on demand deposits. If an individual deposits 100 dollars in Bank A, Bank A may lend $80 of this deposit to another individual, the second individual now has $80 and the bank still has the $100 it obtained from the first depositor, so the money supply has been expanded by $80. Bank B holding the $80.00 will hold 20% of the $80.00 or $16.00 in income and may loan the remaining $64.00 to a third person. Now, the money supply has been increased by an additional $64.00. This process may be repeated until there are no more excess reserves. If the reserve requirement is 20%, the full money expansion is $500, while if the reserve rate is 25%, the money expansion is $400. Thus, the larger the legal required reserve ratio the less the ability of the commercial banking system to expand the money supply, i.e. create money.

**IMPACT OF MONETARY POLICY.** A change in monetary policy will have an unequal impact on business and households. Those economic activities (business and households) that are heavily dependent on credit, such as housing, are especially affected. Monetary policy of the Federal Reserve System along with fiscal policy of the federal government are the two primary tools used in the U.S. to bring about the economic goals of growth and stability. Since monetary policy is determined by the Federal Reserve and fiscal policy by the Federal government, the two may agree on needed economic policy, or the two may disagree and in fact conflict. This condition serves as an important check and balance on the decision makers with the very difficult job of determining appropriate economic policy. There is, however, the possibility that the effects of one policy will be cancelled by the effects of the second policy.

## LIST OF ECONOMIC UNDERSTANDINGS IN CONCEPT AREA VII

1. Money is the most liquid assest an individual or firm can own.

2. Money serves as a medium of exchange as well as a storehouse and measure of value. Most American money is in the form of checking accounts.

3. The quantity equation of exchange explains the importance of the quantity of money in determining the level of real income and the level of prices in an economy.

4. The Federal Reserve System provides flexibility to the money supply and supervises national banks and some state banks. The Fed also inspects the books of the member banks, transmits checks between banks, and holds the major bank account of the U.S. Government.

5. Monetary Policy (the changing of money supply) is directed by the Federal Reserve System.

6. The money supply is changed by the selling or purchasing of government securities to or from the public, (open market operations) by setting the discount rate, and by adjusting the legal reserve requirement for member banks.

7. Each of the tools of monetary policy affects excess reserves held by member banks.

8. The banking system as a whole can create money.

9. A change in monetary policy will have an unequal impact in both the business and consumer sectors of the society.

10. Monetary and fiscal policy are the two primary tools used in the U.S. to bring about the economic goals of growth and stability for the country.

# TEACHING APPLICATIONS IN CONCEPT AREA VII

## University Level Instruction

**Practice with Concept:**

- The Federal Reserve System has redefined the categories used to refer to money. Find out what is included in measures of M1A, M1B, M2, M3, and L.
- Look for articles which tell the size of the money supply. Follow the measures of money supply for several weeks.
- While you are collecting data on the money supply, look for articles on FED policy. Is FED policy related to fluctuations in the money supply? Explain.
- Have you borrowed money recently? Explain how that money affects the general economy.
- Explain how banks create money. When is the creation of money good/bad for the general economy?

**Tight Rope***

The student will be able to understand that:

> *Primary Economic Understanding:* Monetary and fiscal policy are the two primary tools used in the U.S. to bring about the economic goals of growth and stability for the country.
>
> *Secondary Economic Understanding:* Monetary and fiscal policy have to be coordinated in order to be effective.
>
> The functions of the Council of Economic Advisors and the Federal Reserve System can be identified.

*Purpose:* This simulation will help make the student aware of the various decisions involved in developing sound economic stabilization policies. It will also help the student trace the relationship between

---

*\*Tight Rope,* Clinton Hartmann, Education Center, 100 W. Rio Grande, El Paso, Texas 79902.

## 144 Money, Monetary Policy and the Federal Reserve System

monetary and fiscal policy change and some important economic indicators.

*Materials and Instructions:* This is a commercially produced simulation that could be purchased from the publisher.

The class is divided into several separate groups. Each group forms a council of economic advisors and is presented with a data sheet representing a particular time period of U.S. current history. The data sheet includes information on GNP, employment, wholesale and consumer price indices, money supply, federal budget, investment and several other indicators. Each council has a work sheet for each round to help it develop its policy recommendations. The worksheet allows the council to trace the impact of each policy decision on the economy in detail.

*Economic Content and Debriefing:*

1. Not all policy tools should necessarily be used in every situation.

2. Monetary and fiscal policy have to be coordinated in order to arrive at the optimum results.

3. Each economic fluctuation that the U.S. has witnessed has had its own special characteristics and thus required its own unique policy mix.

4. In some cases the best policy to recommend is that no action is necessary.

5. Direct price and wage controls is an alternative policy available for use if necessary.

**How to Cure Inflation**

The student will be able to understand that:

> *Primary Economic Understanding:* Inflation results from a growth of the money supply that exceeds the growth in the production of goods and services.
>
> *Secondary Economic Understanding:* One cause of inflation is a government that has exclusive control of the money supply.
>
> The solution is to slow down the rate at which new money is printed.

*Purpose:* To explain how to return the economy to a healthy state of non-inflationary growth.

## Money, Monetary Policy and the Federal Reserve System

*Materials and Instructions:*

1. Film, How to Cure Inflation, from the Free to Choose film series.*
2. Resource Guide for the film which includes:

   Objectives                       Classroom Applications
   Basic Principles in the film     Terminology
   Discussion Topics                Quiz

*Economic Content and Debriefing:*

1. Inflation is defined as an increase in the average level of all prices with a decline in the purchasing power of money.

2. Inflation results from an increase in the supply of money which causes an increase in the demand for goods and services. Unless the production of goods and services increases with an increase in the supply of money, prices will rise.

3. Government is one major beneficiary of inflation in terms of taxation, for which inflation is a hidden tax.

   Inflation also redistributes resources from the private sector to the public sector without the direction of political leaders.

4. Inflation can destroy an economy because of (a) the uncertainty for making long-run decisions and (b) the lack of a direct relationship of income to the contribution that the resource owners make to production.

5. The side effects from efforts to cure inflation must be identified as periods of higher rates of unemployment, temporarily, and slower growth rates; they are not the cause of inflation.

**Chase Cuts Prime to 20% From 20½% — Newspaper Clipping†**

Students will be able to understand that:

> *Primary Economic Understanding:* The quantity of money in the society affects the level of spending of the country and therefore the general economic health of that society.

> *Secondary Economic Understanding:* Monetary Policy (control of the money supply) must address economic goals of the country that may be in serious conflict.

---

*\*Free To Choose Film Series* by Milton Friedman, WQLN/Public Communication, Erie, Pennsylvania, 1980.

† *Chase Cuts Prime to 20% from 20½%* New York Times, May 30, 1981.

### 146 Money, Monetary Policy and the Federal Reserve System

*Purpose:* The analysis of this article will help students understand that a decrease in the money supply will dampen inflation, but may create other economic problems.

*Materials and Instructions:* Select four to six students to conduct a group study. Have the group select a chairperson. Provide each group member with a copy of the news clipping and a copy of the following instructions for conducting the study.

1. Review the article to:
   a. Define the problem.
   b. Point out the conclusions or goals.
2. Identify the relevant economic principles or concepts.
3. Analyze the alternatives.
4. Choose and support your alternatives.
   a. Point out why you do or do not agree with conclusions of the article.

Allow between thirty and forty-five minutes for group study (over-night assignment is even better); then ask the group or a spokesperson for the group to report the conclusions of the group to the class and lead a discussion with the entire group.

*Economic Content and Debriefing:*

1. The quantity of money in the society affects the level of spending which in turn determines real income, employment and prices.

2. Once the Fed determines the appropriate monetary policy any one of three monetary tools are available to affect the member banks' excess reserves which affects the quantity of money.

3. Economic stability and growth (inflation or recession) are directly affected by the supply of money or the monetary policy of the Federal Reserve System.

# The New York Times

NEW YORK, FRIDAY, MAY 29, 1981

## Chase Cuts Prime to 20% From 20½%

### Interest Rates Down Sharply in Credit Markets

**By THOMAS L. FRIEDMAN**

The Chase Manhattan Bank cut its prime lending rate yesterday to 20 percent from 20½ percent, but many economists and analysts were reluctant to interpret the move as the start of a long-term drop in interest rates.

Treasury Secretary Donald T. Regan, however, predicted in Washington that interest charges were near their peak and said they should decline over the next few months.

"The downturn in the Federal funds rate has only lasted a few days," said William V. Sullivan, senior vice president of the Bank of New York, "and the market has been too volatile of late for people to determine whether this drop is permanent."

None of the country's other major banking institutions followed Chase's lead. Yesterday's fall in the prime reversed a monthlong rise of 3.5 percentage points, which only last Friday brought the key lending rate to 20½ percent.

Interest rates were also down sharply yesterday in the credit markets. The Treasury sold new 13⅞ percent, five-year five month notes at a 13.95 percent average rate, considerbly less than the 14.6 percent yield expected earlier in the week. [Page 31.]

Charles Francis, a spokesman for Chase, said the bank, the nation's third largest after the Bank of America and Citibank, had acted "in response to the recent drop in the cost of our raw material, money." The prime, nominally the rate on short-term loans for the most creditworthy corporate customers, is the base rate banks use to compute interest charges for everyone from its those customers to consumers.

"We have pegged the interest rate lower," Mr. Francis said. "But this is not a prediction of a permanent downturn in interest rates."

Treasury Secretary Regan, however, told a group of businessmen in Washington that interest rates were "somewhere near their peak" and "probably" would be coming down in the next few months.

Commerce Secretary Malcolm Baldridge said at a news conference in the capital that a slowdown in both inflation and the growth of the nation's money supply could bring the prime rate down to 14 or 15 percent by year's end.

In view of the recent volatility in interest costs, leading banking analysts were reluctant to read any long-term significance into yesterday's drop in the prime.

Salomon Brothers' chief economist, Henry Kaufman, whose predictions on the course of interest charges have sent financial markets soaring or skidding, said yesterday that rates would continue to be volatile and that, "on balance, both short-term and long-term rates will move higher."

The prime rate peaked last December at a record 21½ percent. It then slid back to 17 percent in early April, reflecting declines in other interest rates. But resurgent loan demand and the Federal Reserve's efforts to constrain the growth of the nation's money supply eventually forced it back up to 20½ percent level.

Banking analysts cited two reasons for the recent downward pressure on the prime: yesterday's drop in the Federal funds rate, the cost of overnight loans between banks, to around 17 percent after two weeks in the 19-to-20 percent range, and the anticipation of a continued fall in the growth of the money supply in May compared with April.

Some major banks were waiting for the Fed's announcement of money supply figures today for the latest reporting period before adjusting their prime rates, analysts suggested.

148  Money, Monetary Policy and the Federal Reserve System

## Secondary Level Instruction

**The Federal Reserve System**

The students will be able to understand that:

> *Primary Economic Understanding:* In the United States the money supply is regulated by the Federal Reserve System.
>
> *Secondary Economic Understanding:* The Fed, as the Federal Reserve System is called, consists of 12 federal reserve banks and is controlled by a Board of Governors, a group of seven appointed by the President of the United States.

*Purpose:* The student should understand the structure and operation of the Federal Reserve System to control the nation's money supply (monetary policy) in order to promote economic stability and growth in the country.

*Materials and Instructions:*

1. The following graphic organization of the Federal Reserve System should be distributed to every student.
2. Assign two or three students to a particular entry on the chart (A particular rectangle). Ask that the teams prepare a concise statement on the assigned topic.
3. When these reports are completed the teams should report to the class.
4. The teacher will then lead a discussion to integrate the information for the students as well as answer questions.

*Economic Content and Debriefing:*

1. All national banks and some state banks belong to the Federal Reserve System.

2. The Fed controls the money supply by:

    a. Open market Operations: the sale or purchase of government securities between the Fed's portfolio holdings and the general public.
    b. Member banks' legal required reserves: change the percentage of demand deposits that a member bank must keep in cash or as deposits with the federal reserve bank.
    c. The discount rate: change the rate of interest federal reserve banks charge on loans to member banks.

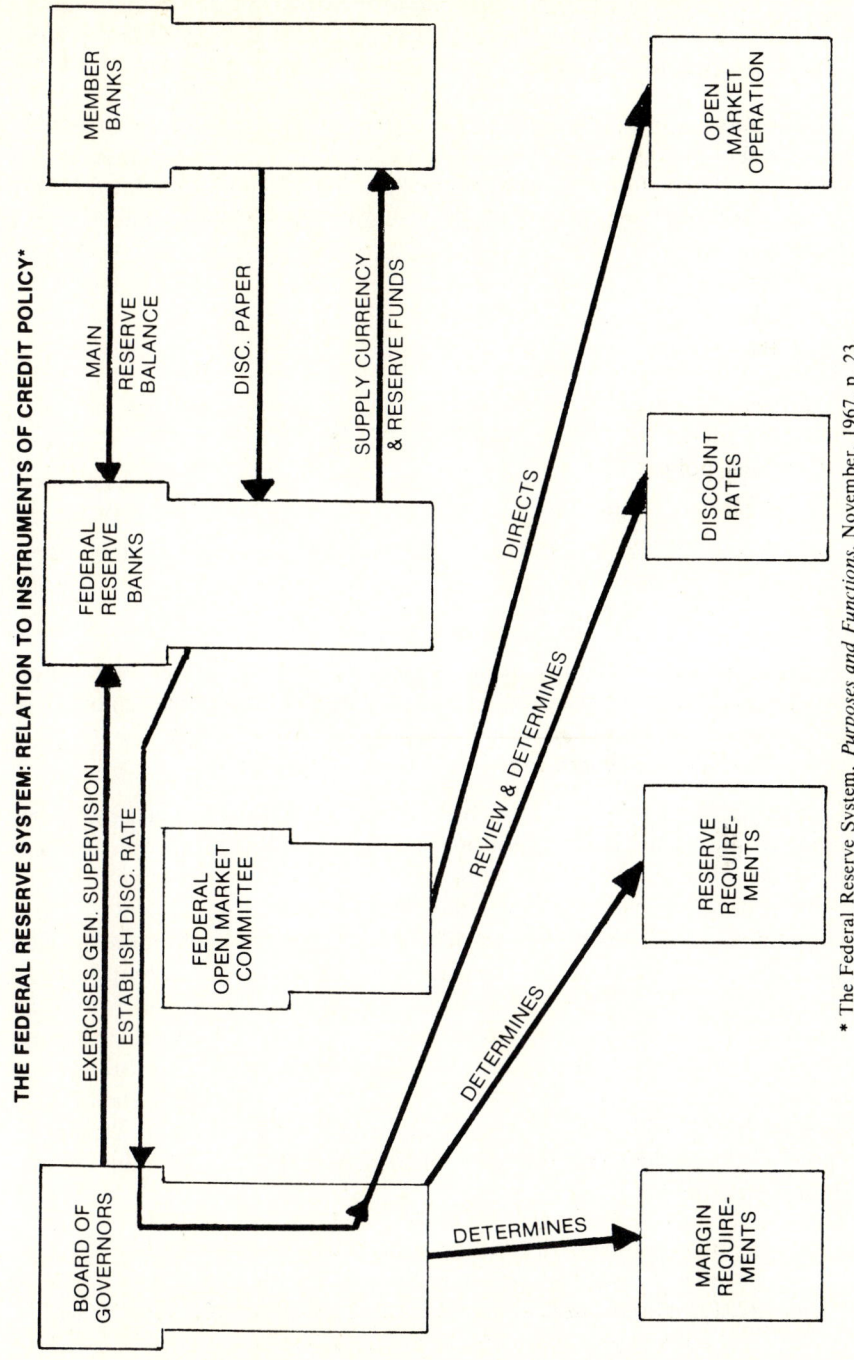

150  Money, Monetary Policy and the Federal Reserve System

     d. Margin requirements: regulate the down payment that must be made when corporate stocks are purchased on credit in the stock market.

3. The tools of monetary policy listed above work through their impact on member banks' excess reserves. If the banks hold large amounts of excess reserves, they are ready to make loans and charge relatively low interest rates. The reverse is also true: low excess reserves means fewer loans and higher interest rates.

**You're A Banker***

The students will be able to understand that:

    *Primary Economic Understanding:* The banking system as a whole can create money by making loans to businesses and consumers.

    *Secondary Economic Understanding:* Monetary policy (the changing of the money supply) is directed by the Federal Reserve System to promote economic stability and growth.

    *Purpose:* This simulation was selected to show the student the importance of the commercial banking system in influencing the quantity of money in the economy. It could also be used to show how the discount rate is used to implement monetary policy.

    *Materials and Instructions:* This is a commercially produced game that could be purchased from the publisher. It includes several complete sets of material so that all of the students in a class can participate in the simulation. The game involves having each group of students form a commercial bank and decide on different applicant's loan requests. Each loan approved creates a certain amount of capital goods, job opportunities, community services and consumer goods. In the second round the feedback on the loans made by the student commercial banks becomes known to the banks and they have to adjust their position accordingly. To simulate the real world, the last round involves the creation of the Federal Reserve Bank giving the student commercial banks the opportunity to either discount their loan holdings, or to borrow directly from the Federal Reserve Bank.

---

*\*You're A Banker,* The Federal Reserve Bank of Minneapolis, Minneapolis, Minnesota 55480, 1975.

*Economic Content and Debriefing:*

1. Banks, through the usual requirement, are able to create money as one bank's loans are another bank's deposits.

2. When banks increase their lending they create new opportunities. This expansion is translated into employment opportunities for the residents of the community.

3. Loan approval is an involved process that entails a subjective evaluation on the part of the banker.

4. Without some control on the monetary expansion and contraction ability of the commercial banking system, the economy would respond in an unstable manner.

5. The discount rate is one way to conduct monetary policy and it involves the creation and destruction of excess reserves for commercial banks.

## Elementary Level Instruction

**How Would You Pay?**

The student will be able to understand that:

*Primary Economic Understanding:* Money is the most liquid asset an individual or firm can own.

*Secondary Economic Understanding:* Money serves as a medium of exchange. Most American money is in the form of checking accounts.

*Purpose:* This activity was developed to make the elementary student aware of the various kinds of money used in the U.S. It will also help the student understand the costs of using alternative ways to pay for a product.

*Materials and Instructions:*

1. Make up a situation where the students have to purchase a particular product and pursue with them the alternative ways of payment. The list should include: currency, coins, checks and credit cards.
2. Look at the other forms of storing money and compare them to the above mentioned means of payment. For example savings accounts, certificates of deposit, and government savings bonds.

## 152 Money, Monetary Policy and the Federal Reserve System

*Economic Content and Debriefing:*

1. Money is what people accept in exchange for goods and services. Each form of money has its advantages and disadvantages.

2. Savings accounts and other forms of time deposits are near money because they are accepted in exchange for goods and services.

3. The cost of using currency or coins is the forgoing interest that could be earned by keeping the money in a savings account or any other interest earning account. This could be developed as the opportunity cost of holding cash.

**Trade-offs, Lesson 9 ("Why Money?")***

The student will understand that:

*Primary Economic Understanding:* Money serves as a medium of exchange as well as a storehouse and measure of value.

*Secondary Economic Understanding:* The two main forms of money are currency or cash (paper bills and coins) and checking accounts (demand deposits).

*Purpose:* This film lesson is designed to acquaint students with the major uses and forms of money.

*Materials and Instructions:* Individual films in the series along with the Teacher's Guide are available from the producer, the Agency for Instructional Television.

Through dramatization of a situation involving barter, the film "Why Money" illustrates the convenience of money as a medium of exchange. The main forms of money (currency and checking accounts) are discussed; the use of credit cards, including how these differ from money, is also explained. Follow-up activities suggested in the Teacher's Guide include discussion questions, a barter game, and other classroom exercises for extending students' understanding of the forms and functions of money and the purposes of voluntary exchange.

*Economic Content and Debriefing*

1. People exchange things because both sides expect to benefit from the

---

*\*Trade-offs* consists of a series of fifteen 20-minute television film programs produced by the Agency for Instructional Television, Bloomington, IND.

trade. Direct exchange without the use of money (i.e., barter) is often inconvenient and time consuming.

2. Money is accepted in exchange for most goods and services. Because of its convenience and general acceptability, money increases the benefits of trade.

3. In addition to making trade easier, money serves as a store of value (i.e., money earned today can be held and spent on some future date) and also as a measure of value (i.e., it expresses value in common units, thereby allowing for comparison of the values of two or more items).

4. The two main forms of money used today are currency (paper bills and coins) and checks. Checks are considered money in that they are backed by a deposit in a bank. Persons receiving checks can endorse them over to others, receive cash for the amount of the check, or deposit the check in their own bank account.

5. Each form of money has its uses and certain advantages. Coins are useful for purchases of less than $1, and for vending machine purchases; paper bills are useful for purchases of larger amounts when cash is the only form of money accepted; checks provide a safe and convenient means for sending money through the mail, for handling large sums, and for record keeping.

## 154 Money, Monetary Policy and the Federal Reserve System

# EVALUATION OF CONCEPT AREA VII

1. Discuss three functions of money.
2. What is the form of a large part of the US money supply?
3. Interpret the quantity equation of exchange.
4. How does the quantity of money relate to the level of employment and economic activity?
5. Is it true a given quantity of money can support only one level of economic activity? Why?
6. What is the purpose of the Federal Reserve System?
7. Describe the structure of the Federal Reserve.
8. Evaluate the techniques used by the Federal Reserve System to change the money supply.
9. What is meant by monetary policy?
10. Explain how the banking system can create money.
11. Discuss the impact on the housing industry of a "tight" monetary policy (reduced money supply and/or increased interest rate).
12. Define the two primary tools in the USA to bring about economic growth and stability.
13. What may be the effect on the economy if at a given time, monetary policy goals differ from fiscal policy goals?
14. Is there an advantage to the economy from separate administration of monetary and fiscal policy?

For reference, use List of Economic Understandings for this Concept Area.

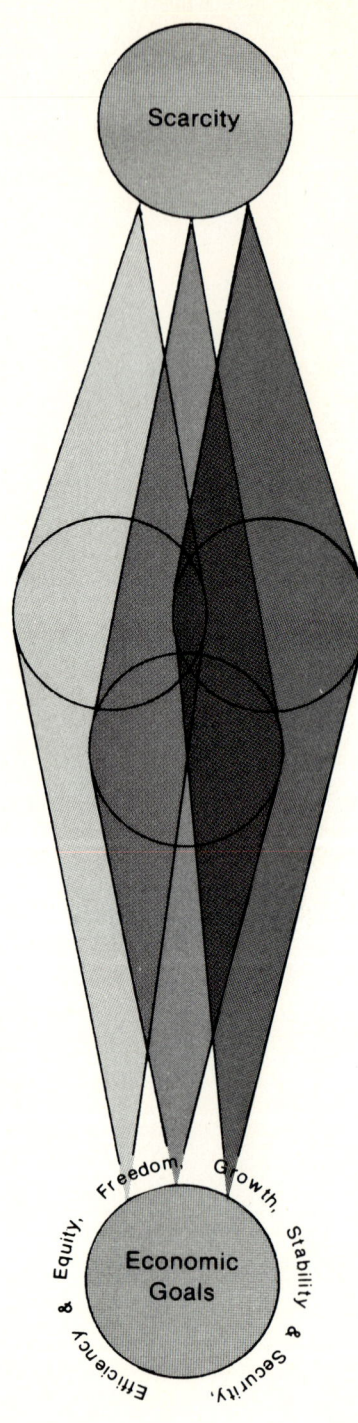

- ● —Personal and Household Finance (Spending and savings program of the household.)

- ● —Producer and Manager of Production (Producer of output and consumer of that output.)

- ● —Director of Public Production (Spending and saving programs—as a citizen in one's democratic role.)

Complete code of screenings for Model on Page 6.

# INTERNATIONAL ECONOMICS

## Concept Area VIII

### Contents

**OVERVIEW OF CONCEPT AREA VIII** — 158

  The World Economy    158
  Reasons for International Trade    158
  Measurements in International Economics    159
  Process of International Trade    159
  International Monetary System    160
  Problems of International Trade    160

**LIST OF ECONOMIC UNDERSTANDINGS IN CONCEPT AREA VIII** — 162

**TEACHING APPLICATIONS IN CONCEPT AREA VIII** — 163

**Universities Level Instruction**    163
  1. Guns and Butter    163
  2. Comparative Advantage    164
  3. Strong Dollar Causes Broad Price Slump—Newspaper Clipping    166

**Secondary Level Instruction**    168
  1. Import    168
  2. Balances in International Trade    169

**Elementary Level Instruction**    172
  1. Where Do They Come From?    172

**EVALUATION INSTRUMENT OF CONCEPT AREA VIII** — 173

## OVERVIEW OF CONCEPT AREA VIII

**WORLD ECONOMY.** International economics addresses itself to two important questions:

(1) Why does trade take place between nations? and
(2) How does trade take place between nations?

The answer to the first question is referred to as the theory of international trade whereas the answer to the second is referred to as international finance. Although the two questions have been traditionally separated in order to simplify their answer, one should be aware that they are closely related.

**REASONS FOR INTERNATIONAL TRADE.** International trade which is justified and encouraged for two reasons, involves the exchange of products between the peoples of different nations. The most obvious but the secondary reason nations engage in foreign trade is explained by the concept of *absolute advantage*. This concept states simply that nations trade the products in which they are superior (more productive) to other nations due to climate, availability of natural resources or even just the innate ability of its people. This concept explains Americans' importation of coffee, cocoa, tea, coconuts, bananas, and a large number of other commodities that either cannot be produced in this country, or if produced the costs would be prohibitive. The concept of absolute advantage explains only a small portion of world trade. The primary reason nations trade is explained by the concept of *comparative advantage*. That is, a nation will benefit if it will concentrate its efforts and production on a particular item or items where it has the greatest advantage relative to other nations and then trade. A nation could therefore produce everything more cheaply than other nations, and find it is beneficial for this nation to specialize in the products where it is relatively more efficient.

To illustrate, suppose a two-commodity, two-nation world existed in which Britain can produce both steel and wine more cheaply than France. If Britain was relatively more efficient in the production of steel than in the production of wine as compared to France, then specialization and trade would profit both nations. It would be to Britain's advantage to specialize in steel production, where it is relatively most efficient, and it would pay France to specialize in wine production, where it has the least disadvantage relative to Britain.

A small country, with few economic resources or products, such as Switzerland or Norway, cannot hope to maintain an adequate standard of living without engaging in international trade. Large nations, such as the United States or the Soviet Union, with diversified resources are less dependent upon international trade than small nations, but likewise fare much better with international trade than without it. Every country depends on international trade to supply some of its material goods and to sell some of its raw materials or manufactured products.

**MEASUREMENTS IN INTERNATIONAL ECONOMICS.** In terms of volume, a country's most important foreign economic transactions are importing (the purchasing of commodities from foreign countries) and exporting (the selling of commodities to foreign countries). The difference between a country's exports and imports is usually called the *balance of trade*. If exports are larger than imports then the country has a surplus in its balance of trade, and if imports exceed exports then the country has a deficit in the balance of trade. The balance of trade however, constitutes only a portion of the country's total international economic transactions. These transactions also include the sale and purchase of services, the sale and purchase of securities such as stocks and bonds, expenditures by tourists, foreign aid by governments, investment by corporations in plants and equipment and many other kinds of international transactions. These transactions are entered in the country's *balance of payments* which is a listing of all foreign transactions between a country's residents and the rest of the world. A surplus in the balance of payments exists when there is a larger inflow of money into the country as compared to the outflow of money from that country. a deficit in the balance of payments would result from a larger outflow of money as compared to the inflow of money. Thus a country can have a surplus in its balance of trade and yet show a deficit in its balance of payments. This means that policy makers should consider all money flows into and out of their country.

**PROCESS OF INTERNATIONAL TRADE.** The "how" does foreign trade take place is as important as the "why" does foreign trade take place.

The value of a country's currency in terms of other currencies is referred to as the *exchange rate*. The exchange rate is the price of currency. It is determined by the supply and demand for the particular currency. The supply of a currency is determined by the outflow of money from the country (imports) and the demand for the currency by other countries (exports). Therefore, if a country has a persistent deficit in its balance of payments, i.e. the outflow of money is larger than the inflow of money, its currency's exchange rate will decline. This will mean that the value of its currency in terms of other currencies will decline, thereby causing its imports to be relatively more expensive for its residents and its exports relatively cheaper for its trading partners. This will stimulate exports and curtail imports improving the deficit in the balance of payments. If, on the other hand, a country has a surplus in its balance of payments, i.e. the inflow of money is larger than the outflow of money, its currency's exchange rate will increase. This will mean that its currency will become more expensive in terms of other currencies, thus making its imports relatively cheaper for its residents and its exports more expensive for its trading partners. This will increase imports and reduce exports, decrease the surplus and possibly eliminate it in the balance of payments.

**INTERNATIONAL MONETARY SYSTEM.** The determination of exchange rates is very important; it influences a country's trading relationships with the rest of the world. Therefore, the need for a comprehensive *international monetary system* to determine exchange rates is paramount. After World War II the world followed a system of fixed exchange rates, usually referred to as the Bretton Woods System or the Gold Exchange System. This international monetary system had all exchange rates fixed to the dollar and the dollar in turn had a fixed value in terms of gold. These exchange rates were changed by international agreement only when persistent balance of payments problems arose. However, as the U.S.'s balance of payments position worsened over the years the countries of the world had to absorb the excess supply of dollars on the foreign exchange market in order to continue to maintain the prearranged fixed exchange rates. This process could not continue indefinitely. As the holdings of dollars abroad increased, foreign governments started exchanging their dollar holdings for gold at an alarming rate. This impact forced the U.S., in 1971, to discontinue its dollars for gold policy. This decision and the continuing deficit in the U.S. balance of payments resulted in the collapse of the Bretton Woods system in 1973. Today a *mixed system of flexible and fixed exchange rates* dominates the world. Under the current system the forces of the market, i.e., supply and demand, determine the relationship between currencies in general with the monetary authorities occasionally interferring in order to guarantee some stability in foreign exchange rates.

International monetary relations between nations are monitored by the *International Monetary Fund (IMF)* which was established after World War II by the free nations of the world. Today, the IMF helps nations correct balance of payments problems without interfering with the flow of trade. This is done by extending credit to deficit countries and forcing surplus countries to bear some of the burdens of adjustment.

**PROBLEMS OF INTERNATIONAL TRADE.** It is recognized by most policy makers that free trade benefits all countries of the world; the economic principle of "specialization" works in the same way between countries as between individuals and/or between regions in a single country. This however has not set aside two main arguments for at least some restriction of trade. The first is based on *national defense.* During major wars, international trade is often severely disrupted. It is possible, therefore, for a country to be cut off from its sources of strategic supplies. The second objection to free trade, known as the *infant industry* argument, states that unless a new industry is protected in a country against world competition long enough to get established the country will never know whether it has a comparative advantage in that product. Both arguments may be criticized as economically unsound, however they do have some political merit.

Restricting trade is one way by which a country could correct a deficit in its balance of payments. It could impose a *tariff* (a tax or "duty" assessed against imported products) thus increasing the price of imported products. It could also set a *quota* which is a physical restriction on the number of units of a particular product allowed to enter the country. Both policies result in a reduction of imports which is reflected in the balance of payments as a decline in out-payments from the country. The world community through cooperation under the General Agreement of Tariffs and Trade (GATT) has generally discouraged and reduced trade restrictions. Countries with balance of payments deficits are encouraged to follow alternative policies to correct the deficit. Many countries have reduced trade restrictions, even with balance of payments deficits, and subsequently realized tremendous growth in international trade.

## LIST OF ECONOMIC UNDERSTANDINGS IN CONCEPT AREA VIII

1. International Economics answers the questions of why and how does trade take place between nations.

2. Nations engage in foreign trade because of the existence of absolute and comparative advantage.

3. International trade benefits all nations participating.

4. A country's balance of trade is the difference between its merchandise exports and imports. It is a part of the country's balance of payments.

5. A country's balance of payments relates the inflow of money to the outflow of money between that country and the rest of the world.

6. A serious deficit in the balance of payments cannot be maintained indefinitely.

7. The exchange rate of a currency is its value in terms of other currencies.

8. There are two kinds of international monetary systems to determine exchange rates:
    a. a fixed exchange rate system
    b. a flexible exchange rate system

9. Economists refute all arguments for trade restrictions as economically unsound.

10. Quotas and tariffs are the most common means of restricting trade.

# TEACHING APPLICATIONS IN CONCEPT AREA VIII

## University Level Instruction:

### Guns and Butter*

The student will be able to understand that:

> *Primary Economic Understanding:* International trade benefits all nations involved in it.
>
> *Secondary Economic Understanding:* A stable international monetary system is a necessary condition for trade to grow between nations.
>
> Common markets are international agreements between countries that allow the free movement of goods between them.

*Purpose:* This simulation introduces the students to the benefits of trade, trade agreements and the conflicts that could develop between nations.

*Materials and Instructions:* This is a commercially produced game that could be purchased from the publisher. It includes all the necessary material to set up a world consisting of five countries endowed with different resources. These resources consist of health, education and welfare, agriculture and industry. Each country may transform its resources from industry into arms as the game progresses. Decisions in each country are performed by a council of ministers consisting of five students. The council has to negotiate trade agreements, form alliances, form common markets and decide on their international relationships with other countries. War is a possible outcome in this simulation, however all sides lose if war breaks out.

*Economic Content and Debriefing:*

1. The concept of opportunity cost will become evident to the students every time they make a decision to switch resources from one category to another. The cost of tying up resources in arms is the forgone use of these resources in industry.

---

*\*Gun and Butter,* by William A. Nesbitt, Simile II, P.O. Box 910, Del Mar, California 92014, 1972.

## 164   International Economics

2. The rules of the game are set up to reward nations when they trade. This is an extension of the argument that trade is beneficial for all parties involved.

3. Forming a common market with other countries results in increasing the resources of each participant by 20%. This is made possible only by international trade. The game makes possible a careful development of the concept of comparative advantage and the benefits of international trade.

4. War is a possibility that involves a reduction in the standard of living of all countries involved.

**Comparative Advantage:**

The student will be able to understand that:

*Primary Economic Understanding:* International trade benefits all countries involved.

*Secondary Economic Understanding:* Even though one country might be superior to its trading partners in all products produced and traded, it will still benefit from international trade if it specializes in the products in which it has the most superiority.

*Purpose:* This activity makes the student aware that the benefits of international trade occur to all countries involved.

*Materials and Instructions:*

1. This activity involves the establishment of two countries that produce just two products. One country will be relatively more superior (its workers more productive) than the other country in the production of both products. Labor is the only factor of production and is transferable from producing one product to the other. Each country has the same number of workers.

2. An example of the activity

|  | Pairs of shoes per worker | Loaves of bread per worker |
|---|---|---|
| U.K. | 1 | 2 |
| U.S. | 2 | 6 |

Assign each country with 100 workers. Have the students determine the output of each country if they have 50 workers producing each product. Add both country's output to determine the total world output of both products before specialization.

For U.K.  50 x 1 = 50 pairs of shoes
          50 x 2 = 100 loaves of bread

For U.S.  50 x 2 = 100 pairs of shoes
          50 x 6 = 300 loaves of bread

Total world ouput  50 + 100 = 150 pairs of shoes
                   100 + 300 = 400 loaves of bread

3. Applying the concept of comparative advantages the U.S. should specialize in the production of bread and the U.K. in the production of shoes.

    With specialization the U.K. will produce 100 x 1 = 100 pairs of shoes and zero bread. The U.S. will produce 100 x 6 = 600 loaves of bread and zero shoes. Thus, world output will be 100 pairs of shoes and 600 loaves of bread.
4. Comparing total world output before and after specialization shows that the world has gained 200 loaves of bread and lost 50 pairs of shoes.
5. In the U.K. 50 pairs of shoes are equivalent to 100 loaves of bread, therefore from the British perspective world output has increased by 100 loaves of bread.
6. In the U.S. 50 pairs of shoes are equivalent to 150 loaves of bread, therefore from the American perspective world output has increased by 50 loaves of bread.
7. If both countries specialize and trade, then this extra realized output would benefit both countries by allowing them more goods to consume.

*Economic Content and Debriefing:*

1. The U.S. is superior to the U.K. in the production of both bread and shoes, however, its comparative advantage lies in the production of bread. This could be seen directly from the table. Compared to the British laborer, the typical American worker is three times more productive in the production of bread but only twice as productive in the production of shoes.

## 166 International Economics

2. Specialization according to the concept of comparative advantage increases the total output available for consumption. The increase will depend on which country's substitution ratio between the two products is adopted. The British substitution ratio is 2 loaves of bread per 1 pair of shoes. The American substitution ratio is 3 loaves of bread per 1 pair of shoes. These substitution ratios are derived from the alternative outputs available to each worker in each country.

3. The actual trade exchange ratio between the two countries will depend on the demand conditions in each country. The closer it is to a particular country's domestic exchange ratio, the smaller will be that country's benefit from trade. This could be seen directly from the example by selecting the U.K.'s domestic exchange ratio and having trade occur between the two countries accordingly.

4. The activity could be complicated further by introducing different currencies and an exchange rate for the currencies. However this adds little to the value of the activity.

### Strong Dollar Causes Broad Price Slump—Newspaper clipping*

The student will understand that:

*Primary Economic Understanding:* A country's foreign exchange rate is determined by the supply and demand for the currency.

*Secondary Economic Understanding:* When a country's exchange rate declines its imports become relatively more expensive for its residents and it exports relatively cheaper for its trading partners.

*Purpose:* The student will understand that a flexible foreign exchange rate permits the value of a country's currency to fluctuate as the price of a commodity fluctuates against the supply and demand of that currency.

*Materials and Instructions:* Select four to six students to conduct a group study. Have the group select a chairperson. Provide each group member with a copy of the news clipping and a copy of the following instructions for conducting the study.

---

**Strong Dollar Causes Broad Price Slump as Traders Fret Over Weak U.S. Exports* Reprinted by permission of Wall Street Journal, Dow Jones & Company, Inc. June 5, 1981.

## 32 THE WALL STREET JOURNAL, Friday, June 5, 1981

# Commodities
## Strong Dollar Causes Broad Price Slump As Traders Fret Over Weak U.S. Exports

By ANNE MACKAY-SMITH
And NEIL BEHRMANN
*Staff Reporters of* THE WALL STREET JOURNAL

The dollar is riding high in currency markets, and many commodity prices are slumping as a result.

Traders fret that U.S. exports may become less competitive in world markets, while producers in other countries will be encouraged to sell more because they can get more local currency for their output.

"The dominating factor in all major markets is currencies," says Jack Boyd, director of commodity research for Drexel Burnham Lambert Inc. in New York. The effect of the dollar's strength may be "more widespread than people think," he adds. Many commodities fell to lifetime lows yesterday, including gold, soybeans and cocoa.

In London, commodity prices have remained steady as the pound sterling has slumped. Normally, those sterling-denominated prices rise as the pound falls, but buyers have been deterred by high interest rates and Europe's recession, London analysts say, so prices in dollars have fallen instead.

Exports of U.S. agricultural commodities could be hurt, analysts say, because they would compete with produce from Europe, Argentina and elsewhere, which are priced in cheaper currencies. "There will be a tendency for buyers to shop for the cheapest country to buy from, and that will depend on the currency they demand for payment," says Ray Worseck, director of commodity research for A.G. Edwards & Sons in St. Louis.

On the other hand, U.S. importers of agricultural and other commodities can look for lower foodstuffs prices. African producers of cocoa, for example, have been encouraged to sell more because, with a stronger dollar, they receive more local currency for their product; this has added to the glut of cocoa and further depressed prices.

In London, where the pound has fallen sharply against the dollar this week, prices on the London Metal Exchange have risen only modestly. "Prices are flat because traders expect the Bank of England to raise interest rates to protect the pound," says Peter Gignoux, a vice president in E.F. Hutton & Co.'s London office.

High U.S. interest rates have been a major force in propelling the dollar higher in currency markets; overseas residents have found it profitable to invest in dollar-denominated instruments. The economic slowdown in Europe, the election of a Socialist president in France and anticipated lower prices for Britain's oil exports have combined to weaken European currencies. High interest rates generally dampen speculation by making it more expensive to own commodities and providing high-yielding alternate investments.

The sharp appreciation of the dollar is affecting European demand for raw materials, analysts note. Common Market countries have raised their own interest rates, and that has postponed economic recovery and hindered demand for metals and other commodities.

"European zinc producers have been offering discounts because their metal is priced in dollars and demand is very weak," comments Christopher Stobart, a director of London's Commodity Research Unit Ltd., a consulting firm.

"About 70% of Common Market soybean imports come from the U.S. and there are signs that they are falling," notes Dipak Shah, an economist for Primary Commodity Research Ltd. in London, adding that Brazilian soybeans might become more competitive.

"Just follow the currencies, that's what commodity prices are doing," says a New York sugar analyst. In recent months, exchange rates and interest rates have played a larger part in futures price movemens than supply and demand for the commodities themselves, says Bill Byers, director of commodity research for Bear Stearns & Co.

On the Chicago Mercantile Exchange's International Monetary Market, trading in currency futures has jumped as speculators have sought to profit from the dollar's strength. Some traders think a reaction might be in store, though. "Everybody is selling" foreign currencies, says Jerry Day, a currency analyst for Shearson Loeb Rhoades Inc. "That's the time when it turns and goes the other way."

One commodity that often falls when the dollar is strong is gold, which dropped $4.60 to $465.20 an ounce yesterday on the New York Commodity Exchange for June delivery. During the day it traded at $459, its lowest level in three months.

"The reason why we had a big bull market in gold in 1979 was the lack of confidence in the dollar and high inflation," notes Howard Levine, A trader at ACLI International Commodity Services Inc. in White Plains, N.Y. As interest rates have risen and investors can earn high returns on dollar-denominated instruments, "gold has come to be regarded as a sterile asset," he says.

1. Review the article to
    a. Define the problem
    b. Point out the conclusions or goals
2. Identify the relevant economic principles or concepts.
3. Analyze the alternatives.
4. Choose and support your alternatives.
    a. Point out why you do or do not agree with conclusions of the article.

Allow between thirty and forty-five minutes for group study (overnight assignment is even better); then ask the group or a spokesperson for the group to report the conclusions of the group to the class and lead a discussion with the entire group.

*Economic Content and Debriefing:*

1. The supply of a currency is determined by the outflow of money from the country and its demand by the inflow of money into the country. Therefore if the ouflow of money is larger than the inflow of money, its currency's exchange rate will decline.

2. If the exchange rate declines, the country's imports are relatively more expensive for its residents. Therefore, fewer imports will be purchased and the balance of payments of the country should improve (everything else held constant).

3. When the exchange rate of one country declines the export level of its trading partners will (everything else held constant) decline. The country itself should experience an increase in its own exports.

4. Foreign Exchange rates are very important for they influence the trading activity of the world and the operation of the concepts of comparative and absolute advantage.

## Secondary Level Instruction

**Import***

The student will be able to understand that:

*Primary Economic Understanding:* International trade benefits all nations involved in it.

*Secondary Economic Understanding:* Nations engage in foreign trade for absolute advantage and comparative advantage.

---
* *Import,* by Elaine Beckett, SIMILE II, P.O. Box, 910, Del Mar, California 92014, 1972.

*Purpose:* This simulation increases the student's awareness of the interdependence between nations and the benefits of international trade.

*Materials and Instructions:* This is a commercially produced simulation that can be purchased from the publisher. It divides the class into several countries and assigns each group of students the task of importing eight different products from at least three countries that they can resell at a profit.

*Economic Content and Debriefing:*

1. In the process of matching countries with products the students will be able to increase their awareness of the various areas of specialization of different countries and regions.

2. The U.S. imports products from other countries, which *can* produce them more efficiently. This point could be explained and used to explain the concept of comparative advantage.

## Balances in International Trade*

The student will be able to understand that:

> *Primary Economic Understanding:* The flow of money across national boundaries in International Trade is an extension of the flow of money in domestic trade in terms of receipts and payments.
>
> *Secondary Economic Understanding:* The Balance of Trade is the net flow of money in exchange for the export of goods and the import of goods. The Balance of Payments is the net flow of money to include all receipts and payments for services, gifts, investments, foreign aid, defense, etc. as well as goods.

*Purpose:* Explain the factors that contribute to a favorable or unfavorable Balance of Trade and Balance of Payments.

*Materials and Instructions:*

1. Students construct a jig saw puzzle to be used for review or by other class members.
2. Each student will write a transaction in International Trade on a separate card. Group the transactions for goods that are imported or exported to represent Trade. Group the other transactions to represent Payments to the U.S. or to a foreign country.

---

*The Balance of Payments, Federal Reserve Bank of Philadelphia, *Series for Economic Education.*

## 170 International Economics

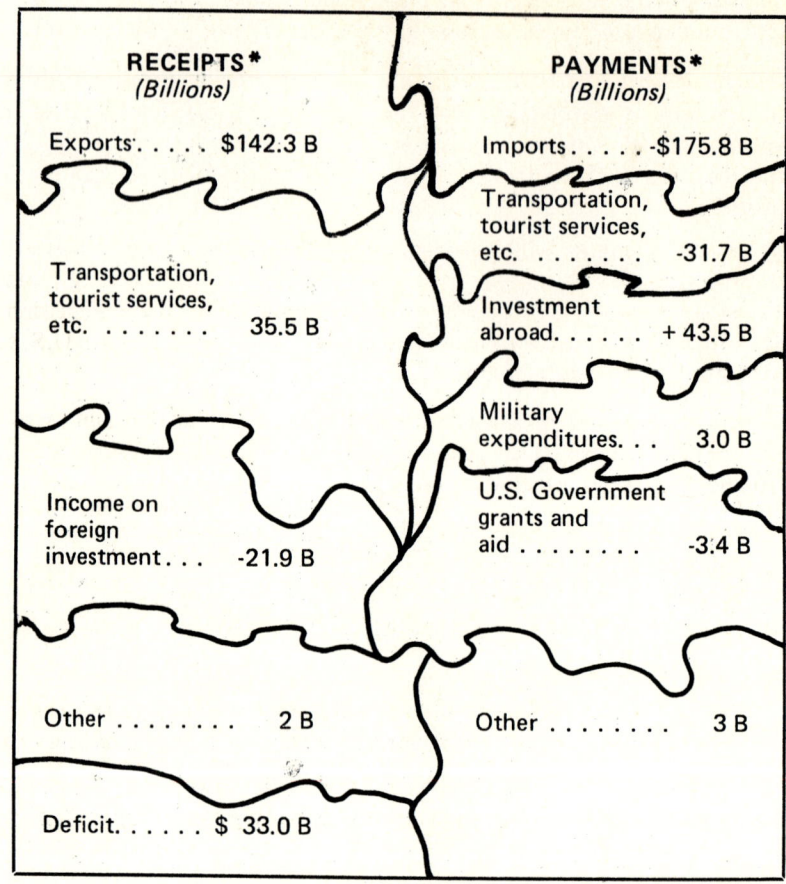

3. Sort the transactions for Trade according to imports and exports for which money is paid or received. Calculate the balance: Exports minus Imports. Label this amount Balance of Trade.
4. Sort the remaining transactions according to receipts or payments in the flow of money to or from the U.S.
5. Arrange the cards for the exports of goods and the receipts of money for other transactions under RECEIPTS.
   Arrange the cards for the imports of goods and the payments of money for other transactions under PAYMENTS.

---

*U.S. Department of Commerce, Bureau of Census, *Statistical Abstract of the United States*, 1980, p. 860.

## International Economics

    6. Total the RECEIPTS and PAYMENTS columns. Find the net and label it, Balance of Payments.

    7. Cut the cards in myriad shapes (each transaction is on a separate part of the puzzle) to fit for a jig saw puzzle. Separate and put in a box to illustrate the general lack of order for understanding the composition of International Trade which prevents analysis.

*Economic Content and Debriefing:*

The student can become aware of the wide range of flows of money across national borders. By grouping the flows into Receipts and Payments, the composition of the Balance of Trade and Balance of Payments can be (a) explained and (b) identified as favorable or unfavorable to the U.S. trade balance.

The Balance of Trade and Balance of Payments can be compared and analyzed.

The Analysis can be projected to;
— the study of exchange rates
— the justification for an unfavorable balance
— the political influences on these balances

Include cards for the following transactions and classify according to receipts, payments, neither.

1. A U.S. firm dealing in the sale of manufactured goods to Brazil hired a Dutch merchant ship to carry goods from a U.S. port to Rio de Janeiro at a cost of $10,000.

2. A Brazilian coffee company hired a German cargo ship for $15,000 to carry a shipload of coffee beans to the U.S.

3. Mr. and Mrs. Mason spent $2,500 for a vacation to Europe:
    $1,400 - tickets on an American airline
    $1,100 - hotel, theaters, souvenirs, and rented cab
    $ 600 - refund for cancelled airline ticket to return via German liner

4. On the same ship as the Masons was a French historian who was coming to the U.S. to study American views of the French Revolution. While in the U.S. he spent 1500 francs ($306) per month.

5. In some areas of the world where no U.S. troops are stationed our national interests are safeguarded by troops of nations such as Greece and Turkey. These nations received $424M worth of U.S. armaments as part of our military aid program.

6. Joan Schultz, a U.S. resident, bought $10,000 worth of shares in a British firm, Imperial Chemical Industries. She received an annual dividend check of 180 pounds ($496).

## Elementary Level Instruction

**Where Did They Come From?**

The student should be able to understand that:

> *Primary Economic Understanding:* International trade benefits all nations involved in it.
>
> *Secondary Economic Understanding:* Nations engage in foreign trade due to absolute and comparative advantage.

*Purpose:* This activity was developed to increase the elementary student's awareness of international specialization and the interdependence of nations through international trade.

*Materials and Instructions:*

1. Develop a worksheet that requires the students to list ten items they use at home which are made in foreign countries.
2. Have each student work independently or in groups to fill their worksheet. For younger students the parents could be used to assist the student.
3. List the names of the products and their country of origin using the worksheets on the chalkboard.

*Economic Content and Debriefing:*

1. Even though the U.S. is relatively less dependent than other countries on the rest of the world for the goods and services it consumes, still these goods are rather evident in our daily lives.

2. In order to be able to import all these goods, we export our own manufactured goods. Therefore, international trade is a two-way relationship that involves both imports and exports.

3. An example of goods we import are cars, televisions, tape recorders, cameras, coffee, mangoes, etc. . . Examples of goods we export are machines, computers, airplanes, wheat, etc.

4. Even though we might be more efficient than our trading partners in producing particular products, for example shoes, it is more beneficial for us to specialize in the items which we have the greatest advantage such as computers.

# EVALUATION OF CONCEPT AREA VIII

1. Explain the two major reasons why nations take part in free international trade.

2. Differentiate between comparative advantage and absolute advantage.

3. How can an underdeveloped nation benefit from international trade?

4. What is a foreign exchange rate?

5. Differentiate between balance of trade and balance of payments.

6. Explain how a country can have a balance of payments deficit and a balance of trade surplus at the same time.

7. How does a depreciation in the value of a currency help correct a balance of payments deficit? What causes the currency to depreciate?

8. For what reason after World War II did the free world follow a fixed rate of exchange for international trade?

9. What are the advantages and disadvantages of a flexible exchange rate system in international trade?

10. Describe the character and purpose of the International Monetary Fund.

11. Identify and evaluate two arguments against free international trade.

12. Describe two techniques to restrict free international trade.

For reference, use List of Economic Understandings for this Concept Area.

# EPILOGUE

One cannot grasp or understand the American economic mechanism without a knowledge of economics. Further, economic understanding or economic literacy requires both a mastery of economic principles and their relationship with each other as well as an ability to apply the principles and to learn to analyze policy issues systematically.

This text attempts to include both these dimensions in a particular way for the university or college education majors as a pre-service or as an in-service elementary or secondary teacher. The structure of the textbook presents the overlapping economic roles of the individual as three: personal and household finance, producer and manager of production and director of public production. The complexities of economics are stripped away by writing and teaching from eight simplified yet comprehensive economic concept areas. The study of each concept area includes: an outline, an overview, a list of economic understandings, university level and pre-university level applications and an evaluation instrument. Finally, each application in a concept area includes the primary and secondary understandings, purpose, materials and instructions for the activity, the economic content and debriefing of the activity.

One last word is needed. The American market system is centered in the individual; we must therefore come to grips with ourselves. The formal organization of society into its political and economic system is totally dependent upon the attitudes of its citizens. Our political and economic system can act only within the framework of attitudes and beliefs which are dominant in the country. The phenomenon of Nazi Germany could never have occured if Hitler and Goebbles had not conditioned the minds of the German people to believe in Aryan superiority and the destiny of that race to rule the world.

The success of a system in a free society is equally dependent upon the attitudes of the people. Four attitudes such as self-reliance, self-discipline, respect for law, and respect for private property serve as cornerstones of liberty.

History makes it clear that these attitudes essential to freedom do not arise spontaneously in the human breast. One wishes they did, but they don't. Each new generation has to be *trained* to recognize that self-reliance is an essential part of human dignity. That total dependence is a circumstance of human degradation. Each generation must be taught that chaos results if the laws are not obeyed.

These attitudes described are not to be confused with value judgments. Economists cannot properly or honestly inculcate values or select goals for any society. However, values and goals can be studied and applied in any economics course. The students can learn to integrate their value judgments with economic theory and solutions to problems can be made by the students on the basis of their own individual values and applicable theory. When alternative values and goals are clearly defined, it is possible to encourage the student to establish a hierarchy of goals; to relate that hierarchy to each problem for solution, recognizing the conflicts and the reinforcements that exist among them and the costs of achieving them; and to respect the goals of others similarly arrived at and applied. Value judgments of the economist, if given, must be identified explicitly because they are just that— value judgments and nothing more.

Value-judging is a present and a continuing process of most students. It is better, therefore, for the economist to recognize this condition and to lead such thought in a professional way. To ignore the value judgments of the individual in a choice economy is to misunderstand the tenets for success of the market system.

# GLOSSARY OF TERMS

*Absolute Advantage*—The advantage a nation has over others when it can produce a product with fewer units of the factors of production than are required by other nations. Such absolute advantage rests on specialized resources, skills, and climate conditions of a nation.

*Accelerator*—A greater or accelerated rate of change in investment coming from a given change in output. The accelerator can intensify the swings of the business cycle.

*Administered Prices*—The setting of prices by conscious managerial decision rather than by the impersonal forces of the market. This is characteristic of the imperfect market but cannot exist in pure competition.

*AFL-CIO*—The major American labor union federation, which was formed in 1955 by the merger of the two federations, the American Federation of Labor and the Congress of Industrial Organizations. The AFL-CIO is not a union, but an organization whose members are unions.

*Assets*—The things which a business firm can claim or which it owns.

*Automation*—Extensive technical changes that involve the automatic linking together of successive stages of the productive process and the automatic control of the production process.

*Average Cost*—Total cost (total fixed cost plus total variable cost) divided by the quantity of output.

*Average Propensity to Consume*—The portion of total disposable personal income that is spent on consumption.

*Balanced Budget*—The financial situation in which government usually Federal Government spending in a given year and taxes in the same year are equal.

*Balance of International Payments*—The statement of the amounts of money spent and received by a nation. It includes the balance of trade arising from exports and imports, other sources of money, such as investments by foreign firms, and expenses, such as foreign aid in the form of money gifts.

*Balance of International Trade*—The statement for a nation of the amounts of money it has received for its exports and has spent for its imports. If exports are larger, the balance is traditionally said to be "favorable"; if imports are larger, it is "unfavorable."

*Balance Sheet*—The accounting statement that records the assets a firm can claim and the liabilities that are the claims against the firm by its owners and by outsiders. Assets and liabilities are always equal.

*Bear Market*—A condition in the stock market in which prices decline.

*Board of Directors*—A group elected by a corporation's stockholders to determine the firm's basic policies. The board is legally responsible for the corporation.

*Bonds*—Securities issued by corporations or governments which represent a loan made to the corporation or government and state a promise to repay the bondholder.

*Bull Market*—A condition in the stock market in which prices are rising.

*Business Cycle*—The periodic up-and-down pattern of the economy from prosperity to recession or depression.

*Capital*—Goods which are used to produce other goods.

*Capitalism*—An economic system in which most capital goods are owned and operated by private firms and individuals. The term usually means the same thing as private enterprise.

*Central Bank*—A bank established by a government to regulate the monetary system of the nation. The Federal Reserve is the central bank of the U.S. Central banks deal mainly with other banks and not with the public.

*Collective Bargaining*—The process of employees gathering together, usually through the use of a labor union, to bargain with their employer over the terms of employment.

*Common Stock*—Stock that states no fixed rate of return and gives the holders a residual claim only to the firm's assets in the event of liquidation of the corporation. Other creditors, bondholders, and preferred stockholders have claims on the assets and earnings that must be met before common stockholders get any payment.

*Communism*—An economic system involving government ownership, control and operation of the means of production and distribution. In its political aspects communism demands a one-party system without public debate of issues or free choice among alternatives by voters.

*Comparative Advantage (principle of)*—A nation's greater advantage in producing a particular item on which it may concentrate its efforts and production. Even when a nation has absolute advantage in all products, those products for which its comparative advantage over other nations is greatest are the items on which it should concentrate its efforts and production. Less productive nations should concentrate on those products for which their comparative disadvantage is least. If the nations do this, and trade, total production will be maximized.

*Consumer Price Index*—An indicator of change in the prices of goods and services. It is compiled by the Bureau of Labor Statistics of the U.S. Department of Labor. It is a weighted average of the prices of hundreds of products, from breakfast cereals to automobiles. For the base period the index equals 100. Thus if the base period is 1971, and the index in a later period is 110, consumer prices in the later period will be 10 percent higher, on the average, than they were in 1971.

*Consumption*—Personal spending for goods and services. It also refers to use of the goods and services bought.

## Glossary of Terms

*Corporation*—A business firm created by a charter issued by a state. It is viewed by the law as separate from the stockholders who own it.

*Deficit*—The financial situation that prevails when any spending exceeds receipts; often the term refers to a year's government spending in excess of the year's tax receipts.

*Deflation*—A lowering of the general price level; usually associated with a depression, a reduction in the money supply, or both.

*Demand*—The amount of a good buyers will buy at any one time at each of the various prices that might be charged.

*Depletion Allowance*—A tax-free percentage of gross income allowed firms using up their natural resources.

*Depreciation*—A money amount that represents an attempt to measure regularly (usually annually) the cost of using a piece of capital goods in production. This is the amount the capital good is worn out.

*Devaluation*—Lowering the value of a nation's money in relation to the money of other nations.

*Disposable Personal Income (DPI)*—The money people have to spend or save after personal taxes are paid.

*Dividend*— Periodic payments made by corporations to their stockholders.

*Durable Goods*—Goods, such as appliances, that are expected to last for a relatively long period of time.

*Economic Growth*—An increase in the real gross national product.

*Economics*—The study of effort of human societies to utilize limited resources to satisfy unlimited wants.

*Elasticity of Demand*—The relationship between changes in the price of an item and changes in its volume of sales. If relatively small price changes cause relatively large quantity changes demand is said to be elastic. Inelastic demand results from the opposite condition, where relatively large price changes cause relatively small quantity changes.

*Equilibrium*—Where supply and demand cross is the equilibrium price and quantity in a market system (a condition toward which economic forces tend to move.).

*European Common Market*—The Common Market, or European Economic Community, is made up of West Germany, France, Italy, the Netherlands, Belgium, England and Luxembourg. It was formed in 1957 to become a free trade area in which internal tariffs and other economic barriers are abolished.

*Excess Reserve*—The amount of a bank's vault cash and Federal Reserve Bank reserve account in excess of that required by law.

*Exports*—From the standpoint of a particular nation, the goods that it sells to buyers in other nations.

*Factors of Production*—The human and nonhuman resources that make possible the satisfaction of human wants; specifically land, labor, capital and entrepreneurship.

*Fiscal Drag*—A condition where rising national income generates higher income tax collections, which in turn dampens the rate of economic expansion.

*Fiscal Policy*—Governmental measures designed to affect the level of economic activity through changes in government spending and taxing.

*Fixed Costs*—Costs that do not vary with output.

*Frictional Unemployment*—A minimum amount of unemployment that reflects mainly routine job changes and is consistent with near full utilization of resources and high-level prosperity.

*Fringe Benefit*—Part of an employee's compensation other than regular wages, such as health insurance paid for by the employer.

*Gross National Product (GNP)*—The total amount of final goods and services produced in a nation. It is measured in terms of actual market prices and is usually based on the time period of one year.

*Imports*—From the standpoint of one nation, the goods that it buys from sellers in other nations.

*Inflation*—An increase in the price level. It causes a decline in the value of money and may be associated with an increase in the money supply.

*Innovation*—New products, services, and methods of production that may lead to profit for a firm.

*Interest*—The cost of using borrowed money, as well as the income of lenders.

*International Monetary Fund*—A fund established in 1944, whose member nations can borrow each other's money from the Fund. It is designed to facilitate international trade and minimize international monetary conversion problems.

*Inventories*—Stocks of goods in possession of businesspeople.

*Investment*—Spending for new capital goods. Investment, along with consumption and government spending for goods and services, constitute the three major domestic spending sectors of the country.

*Labor*—The human factor of production that carries out work planned by management.

*Labor Force Participation Rate*—The percentage of the population either at work or looking for work.

*Law of Diminishing Returns*—The general rule which states that when units of a variable factor of production are added to a fixed factor, the extra output that results from the extra units of the variable factor may at first rise, but sooner or later the extra output will fall (diminish), and eventually total output will fall.

*Law of Supply and Demand*—A generalization stating that, other things equal, prospective buyers will usually offer to buy more of a commodity at any one time as the price goes down; other things equal, prospective sellers will usually offer to sell more of a commodity at any one time as the price goes up. In highly competitive markets, price and output will tend to be determined by the point at which buyers' and sellers' offers are alike.

*Liability*—A claim against a business organization or an amount it owes.

*Line and Staff Organization*—The concept in management of a vertical line of authority and responsibility from top management to the production worker with various staff departments that perform services for those in the line organization.

*Long Run*—A period long enough to allow economic adjustments such as changes in the fixed plant and equipment of firms to take place.

*Macroeconomics*—The branch of economics that concentrates on the overall of economic activity, such as the size of national income. Economic wholes or aggregates, such as total employment, are emphasized.

*Management*—The human factor of production that designs the production process and coordinates labor, capital goods and natural resources.

*Margin (Stock Market)*—The amount of cash (or down payment) regulated by the Federal Reserve that must be paid when corporation stocks are purchased on credit.

*Marginal Cost*—The cost of making one additional unit of a product.

*Marginal Propensity to Consume (MPC)*—The fraction of added disposable personal income that will be spent on consumption.

*Marginal Revenue*—The addition to the revenue of a firm that is caused by the sale of one more unit of its product.

*Microeconomics*—The branch of economics that concentrates on individual units and the price, output, and wage decisions of individual firms and workers.

*Mixed Economy*—An economy that combines private enterprise capitalism with some government ownership and regulation of business.

*Monetary Policy*—Governmental measures designed to affect the level of economic activity through alterations in the money supply.

*Monopoly*—The market structure in which there is a single seller. The term is also used to refer to other market conditions in which market power concentrations exist.

*Multiplier*—When an extra dollar of new spending goes into the income stream and passes from person to person, it raises the income of each and also raises total national income by more than the amount of the original new spending. The ratio of the extra income to the initial extra spending is the amount of the multiplier, which is the reciprocal of the marginal propensity to save.

*National Debt*—The total value of government bonds issued and outstanding.

*National Income*—The total income received by the factors of production before tax. It can be calculated by subtracting capital consumption (depreciation) and indirect business taxes from the gross national product, or by totaling wages, profits, rent and interest.

*Natural Monopoly*—A situation in which monopoly is regarded as the most efficient market structure, such as a public utility. The cost of capital resources is high and there is a natural limit to size of market.

*Open-Market Operations*—The Federal Reserve's purchase of government securities on the open market to raise the volume of money in circulation, or the sale of securities to take money out of circulation.

*Opportunity Cost*—The value of the next best opportunity open to the user of a resource or the spender of money besides the alternative which is chosen.

*Personal Income*—Total income, before personal income taxes, received per year by individuals.

*Preferred Stock*—A stock with a stated rate of return and with a right to a dividend before one is paid on common stock. Also the preferred stockholders have a claim on the firm's assets in liquidation before the common stockholders receive any distribution.

*Price-Earnings Ratio*—The relationship between the market price of a stock and its annual earnings per share. If price is $10 and earnings per share $1, the price-earnings ratio would be 10 to 1.

*Principle of Diminishing Utility*—The principle that at a given time a consumer generally finds that each successive unit of a good yields less satisfaction than the previous unit.

*Private Enterprise*—An economic system of private ownership in which markets are relied upon to set prices and thus allocate the usage of resources.

*Productivity*—Physical output in relation to the input of a productive factor. Usually the term refers to physical output per man-hour of labor.

*Profit*—The money left from a firm's sales revenues after all costs have been met. Profit is the source of payment to the fourth factor of production—entrepreneurship.

*Pure Competition*—The competitive structure in which there are many small producers dealing in a standardized product.

*Real Income*—A measure of income that adjusts for inflation. If a person's income went from $2,000 per year to $8,000 per year while prices doubled, we could say that the person's real income went from $2,000 to $4,000 in "constant" dollars with the purchasing power of the original year. This is because $1,000 in the original year would buy as much as $2,000 after prices had doubled.

*Recession*—A moderate economic downturn; less severe than a depression but associated with increases in unemployment and some decrease in output and income.

*Rent*—The income that goes to owners of scarce, nonreproducible natural resources. In popular discussions rent also refers to periodic payments made for the use of buildings and other man-made goods.

*Reserve*—In banking, reserves are the cash a bank holds in its vault or as a deposit in a Federal Reserve bank. Reserve ratios are stated as a percentage of deposits. Required reserves are the amounts required by the reserve ratios required of a bank.

*Resources*—Human and nonhuman items such as land and machines that can be used for producing goods and services.

*Restraint of Trade*—A legal term referring to a case in which several firms fix prices at a high level which reduces the volume of production.

*Short Run*—A period of time too short to allow a firm to change its fixed plant and equipment. It does, however, permit production to be adjusted with existing plant and equipment.

*Socialism*—A term usually referring to an economic system characterized by extensive government ownership and control of the means of production and distribution.

*Stock*—Securities issued by a corporation which represent a share in the ownership of the firm.

*Structural Unemployment*—Unemployment caused by changes in the structure of the economy. It usually results from a decline in demand for the products of some industries such as rayon or a decline in demand for some types of workers such as unskilled ones.

*Supply*—The amount of a good sellers would sell at any one time at each of the possible prices that might be offered.

*Tariff*—A tax on goods imported from foreign countries. It is designed to discourage such imports by raising the prices of the imported goods.

*Theory*—A hypotheses that shows the pattern of the relationship between certain facts.

*Transfer Payments*—A money payment that does not involve production directly.

*Unemployment*—The situation in which there are persons looking for work but unable to find it. It is usually expressed as a percentage of all persons who either are at work or are looking for work.

*Variable Costs*—Cost, like labor and materials, that vary as output varies.

*Velocity of Circulation*—The number of times per year that the average dollar is spent (transactions velocity) or the number of times it enters the GNP (income velocity).

*Wages*—The income share of labor; for a firm, the price or cost of labor.

# BIBLIOGRAPHY

This bibliography provides a list of the commercially prepared games and simulations described in this Book, a list of representative university reading references for each Concept; a selected list of audio-visual materials for teaching economics and a list of some resource agencies of materials for use in economic education classrooms. A typical teaching learning unit concludes the Bibliography.

I. Games and Simulations—*Economics and Instruction*

*Concept I* - Scarcity and Alternative Systems

*Outdoor Endurance Exercise.* Stanford, g. and Roark, A. *Human Interaction in Education,* Boston: Allyn & Bacon, 1974.

*Scarcity and Allocation: An Economic Decision Game.* Rausch, Erwin. Didactic Systems, Inc., Cranford, N.J., 1968.

*Specialization: A Simulation Game.* Fraas, John W. *The OCSS Review,* Vol. 14, no. 1, Spring, 1978.

*The Envelope Factory. Trade-Offs Manual.* Jt. Council on Economic Education, New York, 1978, pg. 148.

*Concept II* - Supply and Demand

*Big Apple Game. Trade-Offs Manual.* Jt. Council on Economic Education, New York, 1978, pg. 156.

*The Stock Market Game.* Avalon Hill Co., 4517 Harford Rd., Baltimore, MD. 21214, 1970.

*Wheat Game.* Teacher's Manual, *Readings in Economics for 12th Grade Students of American Democracy and American Economic Review* (May, 1965), Jt. Council on Economic Education, New York.

*Concept III* - Income Distribution

*Money and Time Adventures.* Lollipop Dragon Series.

*Powderhorn.* Simile II, 1150 Silverado, LaJolla, CA 92037, 1972.

*Settle or Strike: A Union-Management Collective Bargaining Simulation Exercise.* Games Central, ABT Associates, Inc., 55 Wheeler St., Cambridge 02138, 1974.

*Starpower.* Shirts, R. Garry. Western Behavioral Science Institute, 1150 Silverado, LaJolla, CA 92037, 1969.

*Concept IV* - Profits, Savings, and Economic Growth

*Baldicer: A Simulation Game on Feeding the World's Population.* Wilcoxson, Georgeann, Box 1176, Richmond 23209.

*Duopoly,* adapted from *Oligopoly and Merger.* A simple classroom game. *The Journal of Economic Education,* Vol. 2, no. 2, 1971.

*Concept V* - Consumer Spending and Saving

*Budget: A Simulation of the Struggle for Money in the National Budgeting Process.* Kennedy, Charles L. Interact Company, P.O. Box 262, Lakeside 92040, 1973.

*Managing Your Money.* Mutual Insurance Society.

*The Budgeting Game.* Changing Times Educational Service, 1729 H Street NW, Washington, D.C. 20006.

*The Credit Game.* Leswing Communications, Inc., San Francisco.

Concept VI - Government

*Multiplier.* Tuckerman, B. & Tuckman, H. *The Journal of Economic Education,* 1976, Special Issue 3, 3-72.

Concept VII - Money

*How Banks Create Money. Economics Curricular Materials,* Ohio University CEE, Athens, 1978.

*Mr. Banker.* The Federal Reserve, Minneapolis.

*The Money Game.* Leswing Communications, Inc., San Francisco.

*Tight Rope.* Hartmann, Clinton, Education Center, 100 W. Rio Grand, El Paso 79902.

*You're a Banker.* The Federal Reserve Bank, Minneapolis 55480, 1975.

*Mini-Society.* Kourilsky, Reality Systems, Inc., P.O. Box 35188, Los Angeles 90035.

*Running a Snow Shoveling Business—Simulation.* Cleveland Public School System.

Concept VIII — International

*Guns and Butter.* Nesbitt, William A., Simile II, 1150 Silverado, LaJolla 92017, 1972.

*Import.* Beckett, Elaine, Simile II, 1150 Silverado, LaJolla 92037. 1972.

II. University Reading References:

Concept I - The Economic Problem and Alternative Economic Systems

Bowden, E., *Economics Through the Looking Glass,* 1974, Canfield Printing.

Committee of Economic Development, *Japan in the Free World Economy.*

Heilbroner, *Business Civilization in Decline,* W. W. Norton, 1976.

Maddison, Angus, *Economic Progress and Policy in Developing Countries,* (1970), Allen Unwin.

Schumpeter, Joseph, *Capitalism, Socialism and Democracy,* Har-Row.

Smith, Adam, *The Wealth of Nations,* 2 volumes, Dutton.

Tobin, James, "The Economy of China: A Tourist's View", *Challenge,* 1973.

Ward, Barbara, *Rich Nations and Poor Nations,* W. W. Norton, 1962.

CONCEPT II—Supply and Demand

Davenport, *The U.S. Economy.*

Friedman, M., *Capitalism & Freedom,* 1962, 1963, University of Chicago Press.

Friedman, M., *Essays in Positive Economics,* 1953, University of Chicago Press.

Galbraith, John K., *The Affluent Society,* 1970 NAL Rev. Ed., 1971 HM Sec. Ed., 1976 HM 3rd Rev. Ed.

Radford, R. A., "The Economic Organization of a P.O.W. Camp", *Economica,* 1945.

Wallich, Henry, *The Cost of Freedom: A New Look at Capitalism.*

World Research, Inc., *The Incredible Bread Machine.*

Wright, David McCord, *Democracy and Progress.*

*CONCEPT III*—Income Distribution

Bergman, Barbara, "The Economics of Women's Liberation", *Challenge,* 1973.

Chiswick and Oniel, *Income Distribution,* Norton & Norton, 1976.

Galenson, Walter, *Primer on Employment and Wages,* 1970, Phila. Book Co.

Hamilton, David, *Primer on the Economics of Poverty,* 1968, Phila Book Co.

Myrdal, Gunnar, *Beyond The Welfare State.*

Okun, Arthur, *Equality and Efficiency,* 1975.

Thurow, Lester, *Poverty and Discrimination,* 1969, Brookings.

Ulmer, Melville, *The Welfare State—U.S.A.,* An Exploration in and Beyond, 1969. HM.

*CONCEPT IV*—Profits, Savings and Economic Growth

Beckerman, Wilford, *Three Cheers for the Affluent Society: A Spirited Defense of Economic Growth,* Saint Martin's Press, N.Y., 1975.

Galbraith, J. K., *American Capitalism,* 1956, HM.

Leontief, Wassily, et al., *The Future of the World Economy: A United Nations Study,* Oxford University Press, N.Y., 1977.

Medows, Donnella; Medows, Dennis; Randers, J. and Behrens, William, *The Limits to Growth,* Universe Books, N.Y., 1972.

Mishan, E. J., *The Cost of Economic Growth,* 1967.

Schumacher, E. F., *Small is Beautiful: Economics As if People Mattered,* 1973, Har-Row (1974, 1975).

Wolozin, H., Editor, *The Economics of Air Pollution,* 1966.

*CONCEPT V*—Consumer Spending and Saving

Aaker, David A. and Day, George S., *Consumerism Search for the Consumer Interest,* 3rd ed., The Free Press, 1978.

Burda, Edward T. and Harcourt, Bruce Jovanovich, *Consumer Finance,* 1975, HarBrace.

Feldman, Laurence P., *Consumer Protection: Problems and Prospects,* West Publishing Co., 1976.

Fetterman, Elsie and Jordan, Ruth, *Consumer Credit,* Charles A. Bennett Co., Inc., 1976.

Fetterman, Elsie and Klamkin, Charles, *Consumer Education in Practice,* John Wiley & Sons, Inc., 1976.

Fetterman, Elsie and Schiller, Margery, *Let the Buyer Be Aware, Consumer Rights-Responsibilities,* Fairchild Publishing Co., 1976.

Fetterman, Elsie, *Money Management Choices & Decisions,* Houghton Mifflin Company, 1976.

Garman, E. Thomas and Eckert, Sidney W., *The Consumer's World: Buying, Money Management & Issues Report,* McGraw Hill, Inc., 1974.

Mandell, Lewis, *Economics From the Consumer's Perspective,* Science Research Associates, Inc., 1975.

McGowan, Daniel A., *Consumer Economics,* Rand McNally College Publishing Co., 1978.

Miller, Roger LeRoy, *Economic Issues for Consumers,* 2nd ed., West Publishing Co., 1978.

Spellman, Nancy, *Consumers and A Personal Planning Reader (For You and Me).* West Publishing Co., 1976.

Taylor, Jack L. Jr. and Troelstrup, Arch W., *The Consumer in American Society: Additional Dimensions,* McGraw-Hill, Inc., 1974.

Troelstrup, Arch W., and Hall, E. Carl, *The Consumer in American Society,* 6th ed., McGraw Hill, Inc., 1978.

## CONCEPT VI—Government

Bach, G. L., *Making Monetary and Fiscal Policy,* Brookings Institution.

Havemen, Robert, *The Economics of the Public Sector,* 1976, text ed. Wiley, 2nd ed. 1970 Random.

Heilbroner, Robert, *A Primer on Government Spending.*

Havemen, Robert, and Hamrin, Robert, *The Political Economy of Federal Policy,* Harper and Row, 1973.

Keynes, John, *General Theory of Employment Interest and Money,* HarBrace J., 1965.

McKean, Roland N., *Public Spending,* McGraw Hill, 1968.

Pechman, Joseph, *Federal Tax Policy,* 1971, Norton.

Stern, Phillip, *The Great Treasury Raid.*

## CONCEPT VII—Money

Burstein, Peter L., *A Primer on Money, Banking and Gold,* 1968, Phila Book Co.

Fousek, Peter, *Foreign Central Banking,* 1969, Kennikat.

Friedman, Milton, and Heller, Walter, *Monetary V. S. Fiscal Policy,* W. W. Norton and Co., 1969.

Madden, Carl, *The Money Side of "The Sheet".*

Maisel, Sherman J., *Managing the Dollar,* W. W. Norton & Co., 1973.

Meek, Paul, *Open Market Operations,* The Federal Reserve Bank of New York, 1973.

Okun, Arthur, M., *Issues in Fiscal and Monetary Policy: The Eclectic Economist Views the Controversy,* DePaul University Press, 1971.

Shultz, George and Aliber, Robert, *Guidelines: Informal Controls in the Market Place,* University of Chicago Press, 1966.

## CONCEPT VIII—International

Bhagwati, Jagdish N., *The New International Economic Order: The North South Debate,* M.I.T. Press, 1977.

Friedman, Milton and Roosa, Robert, *The Balance of Payments: Free versus Fixed Exchange Rates,* American Enterprise Institute for Public Policy Research, Wash., 1967.

Friedman, Milton, *Dollars and Deficits: Living with America's Economic Problems,* Prentice Hall, N.J., 1968.

*International Economic Relations of the Western World 1959 - 1971, Part II,* Oxford Univ. Press, 1976.

Irgran, James C., *International Economic Problems,* Wiley, N.Y., 1970.

Kindleberger, Charles, Editor, *International Corporation: A Symposium,* M.I.T. Press, Mass., 1970.

Triffin, Robert, *The Evolution of the International Monetary System: Historical Reappraisal and Future Perspectives,* Princeton University, N.J., 1964.

Triffin, Robert, *The World Money Maze: National Currencies in International Payments,* Yale Univ. Press, New Haven, 1966.

III. *Audio Visual Materials for Teaching Economics:*

These are materials selected from the annotated bibliography, *Audiovisual Materials for Teaching Economics* by Charlotte T. Harter, John Farrell, and David Nelson, Center for Economic Education, Oregon State University. It is published by the Joint Council on Economic Education, 1212 Avenue of the Americas, New York, NY 10036, from whom it may be purchased.

The materials below, like all those in the bibliography from which they are drawn, were judged to meet the Joint Council on Economic Education's criteria of being objective, nonpartisan, analytically-oriented, and educationally effective. The bibliography includes materials for all ages, first grade to adult.

The meaning of the abbreviations and symbols, and the addresses of the publishers, are given at the end of the descriptions.

IT'S A CAPITAL IDEA
4 Filmstrips approx. 11 min each   C
WDEMCO                                                    j-s

(1) Capital? What's That?, (2) What's It Good For?, (3) Capital: How Do You Get Some?, (4) It's A Matter of Choices. Uses cartoon art and a caveman character to trace the role of capital and the history of capital formation from primitive societies to the present. Defines the differences and interactions between political and economic systems. Stresses a purely competitive market economy.

PRIMARY ECONOMICS SERIES
4 Filmstrips     color     C     TG
BFA     1972                                  p

An excellent series, popular with teachers and students. Daniel and his black friend Adam deal with situations that 5-9 year olds encounter and discover some economics in this lively, colorful animated series with real children doing the narration.

Filmstrip #1: "Daniel's Birthday: Choosing Goods and Services" What presents will Daniel get for his birthday? His friends tell him that he will get goods and services. Daniel follows them around the neighborhood to find out about goods and services. He learns why different people choose different things. He learns that footballs are goods. And he decides that the best service of all is Mother serving cake and ice cream.

Filmstrip #2: "Michael's Moon Store: Producing Goods and Services" Michael is starting a business. "What is that?" asks Daniel. Michael explains that businesses produce goods and services that people want. Michael will be a producer and make moon goods. Daniel will be a consumer and buy them. Daniel and Adam find a way to be producers too.

Filmstrip #3: "A Collar for Patrick: Buying Goods and Services" Daniel has lost his pet duck, Patrick. Barney, the policeman, finds Patrick and tells Daniel that his duck needs a collar. Daniel learns that collars are goods and goods cost money. He must find out where money comes from. Daniel then finds a way to earn money to buy the collar.

Filmstrip #4: "Adam Builds A Bank: Saving for Goods and Services" Adam decides to start his own bank when his mother takes a new job at the neighborhood bank. He finds several large cartons and cuts windows and a door. He is not sure why his mother has gone to work, then learns that savings are important to his family. Adam has his own ideas about savings and what the neighborhood children will want to deposit in his bank.

FREE ENTERPRISE
2 Filmstrips 24 min.   C or R   TG
PHM    SSSS    1976             s-c-a

Examines the American market place and the changes that have altered the free economy first described by Adam Smith 200 years ago. The program takes a look at ethical as well as economic values of capitalism and assesses its continuing potential to offer fulfillment and financial success to individual entrepreneurs. Free enterprise is looked at in its pure form and the U.S. system is compared to this model.

DEMAND
21 min.
WDEMCO    color    s-c-a

Begins the presentation of economic analysis with an explanation of the law of demand: the more something costs, the less people want of it. In addition to the price-effect, the film illustrates that factors such as wealth, family size, tastes, and type of work also affect demand.

SUPPLY
20 min.
WDEMCO    color    s-c-a

Shows how the amount produced and supplied responds to market price, and how anticipated sales, selling prices, costs, and profits guide a potential producer.

AN ECONOMIC PRIMER: $$$ TO DONUTS
4 Filmstrips    color    C    G    TG    WS
SCHLAT    1975    s-a

This four-part program explores the significance of money, looks at what determines what something costs and why people earn what they do, and explains how every economic system must answer certain basic questions.

MRS. PEABODY'S BEACH
Film    30 min.    color
WDEMCO    1971    j-s-a

A witty story of a teenage boy who forms a surfing business to raise money for his college education. Numerous economic concepts are developed including scarcity, opportunity costs, marginal revenue and marginal costs, fixed and variable costs, law of diminishing returns, diminishing utility, and entrepreneurship. Discussion is recommended after the film to help bring out the economic concepts presented.

IF THE FERGI FITS, WEAR IT
Film    23 min.    TG
WDEMCO    1976    s-c-a

Demonstrates the principles of a competitive market economy as young people discover the problems and profits of operating a T-shirt business. The business faces numerous headaches including defective merchandise, dipping into capital reserves, establishing quality control, having more employees, unions, and zoning law violations; but it manages to turn a $3,000 profit. The film does an excellent job of illustrating basic principles of economics.

WHY FATHERS WORK
Film    14 min.    color    TG
EBEC    1969    p-i

Explains to students why their fathers go to work. Shows why work is important to a family, a community, and a city. Illustrates how labor and services make the many aspects of city life interdependent.

INFLATION
Filmstrip    C or R    TG
GA    j-s

Features interviews with experts, and with citizens affected by inflation; explains its causes, characteristics and social impact. Outlines various means of coping with inflation; examines value conflicts posed by the option of accepting increased unemployment as an antidote to inflation.

PRODUCTIVITY—THE KEY TO BETTER LIVING
(Set II: American Economy Series)
Filmstrip    color    C or R    TG
MGH    SSSS    1971    s-c-a

Explains the difference between production and productivity and how efficient use of the four factors of production—land, labor, capital, entrepreneurship—can lead to higher productivity. Shows that factors have helped the U.S. achieve such a high level of production.

THE ENERGY DILEMMA
Film    18 min.    color
FI    1973    j-s

The energy crisis in North America is purely a matter of people—increasing in number and demanding ever higher quantities and qualities of services and goods. The solution comes back to people. We just may have to limit our energy appetite—use less, demand less. But are we prepared to?

THE OIL WEAPON
Film    50 min.    color
FI    1975    s-c-a

Hardly anyone in the Western world still remembers or even knows there was an earlier attempt in 1967 by the Arab oil producers to use oil as a weapon in their confrontation with Israel. It failed totally and in the West the conventional wisdom became that the oil weapon had been tried, it didn't work, and it could therefore be forgotten. But in the fall of 1973 the Arabs pulled their failed weapon off the shelf; this time it worked so well that even the Arabs were surprised. There has been endless discussion of the oil crisis ever since then.

ECONOMICS AND THE GLOBAL SOCIETY
3 Filmstrips    color    approx. 17 min. each    C    DM    G    TG
N    1975    s-c

(1) The Wealth of Nations

(2) Rich Nations/Poor Nations
(3) Economic Evolution

Stressing world economic development, trade, and interdependence, this set discusses basic economic concepts and examines how alternative economic systems cope with common problems, analyzes the widening disparities between developed and developing world in view of emerging global problems, and explores interdependence and the feasibility of a truly global society.

TRADE-OFFS
15 Television/Film programs of 20 min each    TG
AIT    color    i-j

Fifteen 20-minute color television/film programs in economic education for children nine to thirteen years old.

"Trade-offs" is designed to help students think their way through economic problems and increase their understanding of economics. Using dramatization and special visuals, each of the fifteen programs considers a fundamental economic problem relevant to the daily life of the child, emphasizes the economic principles and reasoning processes involved in dealing with the problem, and introduces similar unresolved problems to stimulate classroom discussion and follow-up activities.

The programs are as follows: 1. Choice (Opportunity Cost)  2. Malcolm Decides (Personal Decision-making)  3. We Decide (Social Decision-making)  4. Give and Take (Trade-offs Among Goals)  5. Less and More (Increasing Productivity)  6. Working Together (Specialization)  7. Does It Pay? (Investment in Capital Goods)  8. Learning and Earning (Investment in Human Capital)  9. Why Money? (Voluntary Exchange)  10. To Buy or Not to Buy (Buyers and Market Demand)  11. To Sell or Not To Sell (Sellers and Market Supply)  12. At What Price? (Market Clearing Prices)  13. How Could That Happen? (Interdependence of Market Prices)  14. Innocent Bystanders (Market Intervention: Reducing Indirect Costs)  15. Helping Out (Market Intervention: Increasing Indirect Benefits).

*Additional Selected Visual Materials:*

FREE TO CHOOSE
10 films    30 min.    color    TG    I, II, III, IV, V, VI, VII, VIII
WQLN    1980    s-c-a

   The programs are as follows: The Power of the Market, The Tyranny of Control, Anatomy of å Crisis, From Cradle to Grave, Created Equal, What's Wrong With Our Schools, Who Protects the Consumer?, Who Protects the Worker?, The Cure for Inflation, How to Stay Free.

PEOPLE ON THE MARKET    I
7 films    19-23 min.    color    TG
WDEMCO    j-s

   The programs are as follows:    I, II, III.
      Wages and Production, Market Clearing Price, Scarcity and Planning, Cost, Property Rights and Pollution, Supply, Demand.

BASIC CONCEPTS IN ECONOMICS SERIES    I, II, III, V
6 filmstrips    color    TG
BFA    p-i

ELEMENTARY ECONOMICS:    CHOICES AND VALUES    I, III, V, VI
6 filmstrips    color    TG
BFA    p-i

WHY PEOPLE HAVE SPECIAL JOBS:
  THE MAN WHO MADE SPINNING TOPS    I
WHY WE USE MONEY: THE FISHERMAN WHO NEEDED A KNIFE    VII
WHY WE HAVE TAXES: THE TOWN THAT HAD NO POLICEMAN    VI
Filmstrips and films    color    TG
LCA      p-i

MAN'S MATERIAL WELFARE    I-VIII
Film    color    TG
Dow      j-s-c-a

FREEDOM 2000    I - VIII
Film    color    TG    WS    DM
USCC      j-s

WORLD WITHOUT MONEY    VII
Film    color
WDEMCO      p-i

ONCE UPON A DIME    VII
Film    color
CF      p-i

CONSUMER CHOICE    V
Filmstrip    color    TG
Proctor & Gamble      p-i

THE ENDLESS SEARCH - THOMAS A. EDISON    III
Film    color
Ohio Edison      j-s-c-a

AT ISSUE: INFLATION    VI
3 Filmstrips    color    TG
SCHLAT      j-s-c-a

ENOUGH FOOD FOR EVERYONE - FOOD, THE ENVIRONMENT AND YOU - JAPAN    VIII
Filmstrip
IER      j-s-c

*Abbreviations used for supporting materials are:*

| | | | |
|---|---|---|---|
| B | Book | R | Record |
| C | Cassette | TG | Teacher's Guide |
| CB | Student Comics | TXT | Student Text |
| DM | Ditto Masters | WB | Student Workbook |
| G | Game | WS | Student Worksheet |
| MM | 16mm film | | |

The first line of the entry contains the title of the AV item. The abbreviations for grade level are p-i-j-s-c-a where p=K-3, i=4-6, j=7-9, s=10-12, c=college, a=adult. If the film or filmstrip is part of a series, the information is recorded on the second line of the entry beneath the title. Otherwise, the second line of the entry gives the media type, the length in minutes, whether it is in color or black and white, and other supporting materials that may have been included. The third line of the entry lists the producer and/or distributor abbreviation, the year of production, and the grade level for which it is applicable. Concept Areas are designated by I through VIII.

# 192 Bibliography

*Alphabetical Listing of Abbreviations Used for Producers and Distributors*

| | |
|---|---|
| AIT | Agency for Instructional TV |
| BFA | BFA Educational Media |
| CF | Counselor Films |
| DOW | Dow Chemical Co. |
| EBEC | Encyclopedia Britannica |
| FI | Films Incorporated |
| GA | Guidance Associates |
| IER | Imperial Educational Resources, Inc. |
| LCA | Learning Corp. of America |
| MGH | McGraw-Hill Films |
| N | Newsweek |
| PHM | Prentice-Hill Media, Inc. |
| SCHLAT | Schloat Productions |
| USCC | United States Chamber of Commerce |
| WDEMCO | Walt Disney Educ. Media |
| WQLN | Penn Communications, Inc. |

*Alphabetical Listing of Producer's and Distributor's Addresses*

Agency for Instructional Television
Box A
Bloomington, IN 47401

BFA Educational Media
2211 Michigan Avenue
P.O. Box 1795
Santa Monica, CA 90406

Encyclopedia Britannica
   Educational Corporation
Instructional and Library Services
425 North Michigan Avenue
Chicago, IL 60611

Films Incorporated
1144 Wilmette
Wilmette, IL 60091

Guidance Associates
757 Third Avenue
New York, NY 10017

McGraw-Hill Films
1221 Avenue of the Americas
New York, NY 10020

Newsweek
Educational Division
444 Madison Avenue
New York, NY 10022

Prentice-Hall Media, Inc.
150 White Plains Road
Tarrytown, NY 10591

Schloat Productions
150 White Plains Road
Tarrytown, NY 10591

Walt Disney Educational
   Media Company
500 South Buena Vista Street
Burbank, CA 91521

## RESOURCE AGENCIES

Academic Games Associated, Inc.
Baltimore, Maryland 21218

Addison Wesley Publishing Company
Melon Park, CA
Our Economy: How it Works.
Clawson

Advertising Council
25 West 45th Street
New York, New York 10036

Alcoa Foundation
Alcoa Building
Pittsburgh, PA 15219

American Bankers Association
Banking Education Committee
1120 Connecticut Avenue, N.W.
Washington, D.C. 20036

American Council on Consumer Interests
238 Stanley Hall
University of Missouri
Columbia, MO 65201

American Economic Foundation
51 East 42nd Street
New York, NY 10017

American Education Publications
600 Madison AVenue
New York, NY 10017

American Enterprise Institute
1200-17th Street, N.W.
Washington, D.C. 20036

American Farm Bureau Federation
100 Merchandise Mart
Chicago, IL 60654

The American Federation of Labor and
Congress of Industrial Organizations
AFL-CIO Building
815 - 16th Street, N.W.
Washington, D.C. 20006

American Home Economics Association
2010 Massachusetts Avenue, N.W.
Washington, D.C. 20036

American Institute of Banking
Consumer Service Department
400 East Ontario Street
Chicago, IL 60611

American Iron and Steel Institute
Public Relations Department
1000 - 16th Street, N.W.
Washington, D.C. 20036

American Petroleum Institute
1271 Avenue of the Americas
New York, NY 10020

American Stock Exchange
86 Trinity Place
New York, NY 10006

Association Films, Inc.
Sears Consumer Information
518 Burlington Avenue
LaGrange, IL 60525

Association-Sterling Films, Inc.
866 Third Avenue
New York, NY 10022

Atlantic Richfield Foundation
515 South Hower Street
Los Angeles, CA 90071

Better Business Bureau - Local and Area

BFA Educational Media
2211 Michigan Avenue
Santa Monica, CA 90404

Better Homes and Gardens
Reader Service - Dept. A
1716 Locust Street
Des Moines, IA 50303

The Brookings Institution
1775 Massachusetts Avenue, N.W.
Washington, D.C. 20036

Bureau of Labor Statistics
Regional Office
84300 South Wacker Drive
Chicago, IL 60606

Bureau of the United States
Budget
Washington, D.C. 20036

The Calvin K. Kazanjian Economics
Foundation, Inc.
251 Danbury Road
Wilton, CT 06897

Chamber of Commerce of the U.S.
1615 H Street, N.W.
Washington, D.C. 20006

Changing Times Education Services
1729 H Street
Washington, D.C. 20006

The Chase Manhattan Bank
1 Chase Manhattan Plaza
New York, NY 10015

Committee for Economic Development
711 Fifth Avenue
New York, NY 10022

Consumer Affairs Office
New Executive Office Building
Washington D.C. 20506

Consumer Information
Public Documents Distribution Center
Pueblo, CO 81009

Consumer Product Information
Coordinating Center
Washington, D.C. 20407

Consumer Product Safety Commission
21046 Brookpart Road
Cleveland, OH 44135

Consumers Union of the U.S., Inc.
256 Washington Street
Mount Vernon, NY 10550

Cost of Living Council
P.O. Box 7075
Congress Heights Station
Washington, D.C. 20032

Council for Advancement of
Secondary Education, Inc.
1201 Sixteenth Street, N.W.
Washington, D.C. 20036

## 194 Bibliography

Council of Economic Advisers
Washington, D.C. 20402

Council for Family Financial Education
Twin Towers
Silver Springs, MD 20910

Council of Better Business Bureaus
1150 - 17th Street, N.W.
Washington, D.C. 20036

Credit Union National Association
Box 431
Madison, WI 53701

Division of Consumer Protection
Department of Commerce
State of Ohio
275 East State Street
Columbus, OH 43215

Dow Jones & Company, Inc.
Educational Service Bureau
P. O. Box 300
Princeton, N.J. 08540

Dun & Bradstreet, Inc.
1290 Avenue of the Americas
New York, NY 10019

E. I. DuPont de Nemours & Company
Wilmington, DE 19898

Educational Service, Inc.
P.O. Box 219
Stevensville, MI 49127
The Spice Series: Choices; Careers

Education Division
Institute of Life Insurance
Health Insurance Institute
277 Park Avenue
New York, NY 10017

Exxon Corporation
111 West 49th Street
New York, NY 10020

The Federal Communications
   Commission's Secretary
Washington, D.C. 20554

Federal Reserve Bank of Atlanta
104 Marietta Street
Atlanta, GA 30303

Federal Reserve Bank of Boston
30 Pearl Street
Boston, MA 02105

Federal Reserve Bank of Chicago
230 South LaSalle Street
Chicago, IL 60690

Federal Reserve Bank of Cleveland
East Sixth and Superior Avenue
Cleveland, OH 44101

Federal Reserve Bank of Dallas
Wood and Akard Streets
Dallas, TX 76222

Federal Reserve Bank of Kansas City
Grand Avenue
Kansas City, MO 64198

Federal Reserve Bank of Minneapolis
South 5th Street
Minneapolis, MN 55480

Federal Reserve Bank of New York
33 Liberty Street
New York, NY 10045

Federal Reserve Bank of Philadelphia
925 Chestnut Street
Philadelphia, PA 19101

Federal Reserve Bank of Richmond
9th and Franklin Streets
Richmond, VA 23213

Federal Reserve Bank of St. Louis
P.O. Box 442
St. Louis, MO 69168

Federal Reserve Bank of San Francisco
P.O. Box 7702
San Francisco, CA 94104

Federal Trade Commission
Washington, D.C. 20580

Firestone Tire & Rubber Company
Director of Consumer Affairs
1200 Firestone Parkway
Akron, OH 44317

First National City Bank
Park Avenue
New York, NY 10022

Regional Office
Food and Drug Administration
11411 Central Parkway
Cincinnati, OH 45202

Food and Drug Information
Distribution and Mailing Unit
200 C Street, S.W.
Washington, D.C. 20204

Ford Motor Company Fund
The American Road
Dearborn, MI 48121

The Foundation for Economic
   Education, Inc.
Irvington-on-Hudson, N.Y. 10533

General Electric Foundation
1285 Boston Avenue
Bridgeport, CT 06602

General Mills Foundation
9200 Wayzata Boulevard
Minneapolis, MN 55440

Good Housekeeping Bulletin Service
BW5 959 Eighth Avenue
New York, NY 10019

Hallmark Cards, Inc.
Kansas City, MO
My Bank Book

Home Economics Education Association
National Education Association
1201 Sixteenth Street, N.W.
Washington, D.C. 20036

Household Finance Corporation
Money Management Institute
Prudential Plaza
Chicago, IL 60601

Industrial Relations Center
University of Chicago
1225 East Sixtieth Street
Chicago, IL 60637

Institute of Life Insurance
Education Division
277 Park Avenue
New York, NY 10017

International Paper Company Foundation
220 East 42nd St.
New York, NY 10017

Internal Revenue Office - Local

International Labor Office
Washington Branch
917 - 15th Street, N.W.
Washington, D.C. 20005

J. C. Penney Company, Inc.
Educational Relations Department
1301 Avenue of the Americas
New York, NY 10019

Joint Council on Economic Education
1212 Avenue of the Americas
New York, NY 10036

Kiplinger Magazine
1729 H Street, N.W.
Washington, D.C. 20006

Learning Corporation of America
711 Fifth Avenue
New York, NY 10022

MacDonald's Corp.
Illinois Council on
Economic Education
Northern Illinois University
DeKalb, IL 60115
Economics Action Pak

Mansfield Chamber of Commerce
Mansfield, OH 44901
Today's Economics

Manufacturers Hanover Trust Company
250 Park Avenue
New York, NY 10017

Marathon Oil Company
Findlay, Ohio 45840
(Attention: Community Relations)

Merrill, Lynch, Pierce, Fenner & Smith
70 Pine Street
New York, NY 10005

Mobil Foundation, Inc.
150 East 42nd Street
New York, NY 10017

Money
Time-Life Building
541 North Fairbanks Court
Chicago, IL 60611

Monsanto Fund
800 North Lindbergh Boulevard
St. Louis, MO 63166

Morgan Guaranty Trust Company
23 Wall Street
New York, NY 10015

The National Association of Manufacturers
of the United States of America
277 Park Avenue
New York, NY 10017

National Bureau of Standards
Washington, D.C. 20234

National Consumer Finance Association
Education Services Division
701 Solar Building
1000 16th Street, N.W.
Washington, D.C. 20036

National Council for Economic
Education for Children
Lesley College
Cambridge, MA 02238
The Elementary Economist. NCEE.
Cambridge

National Council for the Social Studies
1201 Sixteenth Street, N.W.
Washington, D.C. 20036

## 196 Bibliography

National Foundation for Consumer Credit
1819 H Street, N.W.
Washington, D.C. 20006

The National Grange
1616 H Street, N.W.
Washington, D.C. 20006

National Industrial Conference Board, Inc.
845 Third Avenue
New York, NY

New York Stock Exchange
11 Wall Street
New York, NY 10006

Office of Public Information
Federal Trade Commission
Washington, D.C. 20580

Ohio Bankers Association
33 North High Street
Columbus, OH 43215

Ohio Chamber of Commerce
Columbus, OH 43215

Ohio Consumer Loan Association
79 East State Street
Columbus, OH 43215

Ohio Consumer Union League
1201 Dublin Road
Columbus, OH 43215

The Procter & Gamble Fund
301 East Sixth Street
Cincinnati, OH 45202

The President's Committee on
   Consumer Interests
Washington, D.C. 20506

Public Documents Distribution Center
Pueblo Industrial Park
Pueblo, CO 81001

Savings Bank Association
State of New York
60 East 42nd Street
New York, NY 10017

Scholastic Magazine & Book Services
50 West 44th Street
New York, NY 10036

Science Research Associates
259 East Erie Street
Chicago, IL 60611

Sears, Roebuck and Company
Dept. 703 - Public Relations
Consumer Information Services
925 South Homan Avenue
Chicago, IL 60607

Shell Companies Foundation
One Shell Plaza
Houston, TX 77001

Social Security Office - Local

South-Western Publishing Co.
Cincinnati, OH 45221

State Department of Education
The Instructional Materials Laboratory
The Ohio State University
1885 Neil Avenue
Columbus, OH 43210

State Department of Education
Vocational Education Division
Columbus, OH 43210

Superintendent of Documents
U.S. Government Printing Office
Washington, D.C. 20402

Source for publications of:
U.S. Department of Agriculture
U.S. Department of Commerce
U.S. Department of H.E.W.
U.S. Department of Labor
Bureau of the Budget

Tax Foundation, Inc.
80 Rockefeller Plaza
New York, NY

United States Congress,
   Joint Economic Committee
Washington, D.C. 20510

United States Savings and Loan League
221 North LaSalle Street
Chicago, IL

United States Steel Corporation
600 Grant Street
Pittsburgh, PA 15230

The W. E. Upjohn Institute
   for Employment Research
300 South Westnedge Avenue
Kalamazoo, MI 49007

Whirlpool Foundation
North Shore Drive
Benton Harbor, MI 49022

Willoughby Eastlake School District
and ATO, Inc.
2882 Cricket Lane
Willoughby Hills, OH 44902
Classroom Techniques in
Economic Education

## SPECIALIZED CENTERS
### Joint Council of Economic Education

*National Center for Audiovisual Materials for Teaching Economics*
   Center for Economic Education
   Oregon State University
   Milam Hall, Room 157
   Corvallis, Oregon 97330
   (503) 745-3211

*Center for the Development of Economic Education: Junior High School (Grades 7-9)*
   Center for Economic Education
   University of the Pacific
   School of Education
   Stockton, California 95211
   (209) 946-2463

*National Center for Computer or Assisted Instruction Economics*
   Center for Economic Education
   Mankato State University
   Department of Economics
   Mankato, Minnesota 56001
   (507) 389-2711

*National Repository and Specialized Center for Materials on World Economics*
   Center for Economic Education
   College of St. Thomas
   2115 Summit Avenue
   St. Paul, Minnesota 55105
   (612) 647-5655

*National Center for Personalized Instruction in Business and Economics*
   Center for Business and Economic Education
   Empire State College (S.U.N.Y)
   P.O. Box 130
   Old Westbury, New York 11568
   (516) 997-4700

*National Depository for Children's Stories in Economics*
   Center for Economic Education
   St. Cloud State University
   College of Business
   St. Cloud, Minnesota 56301
   (612) 255-2157

*National Center for the Improvement of Instruction and Curriculum Development in the Teaching of Economics*
   Center for Economic Education
   Illinois State University
   Normal, Illinois 61761
   (309) 438-2439

*National Specialized Center for Business Education*
   Virginia Commonwealth University
   School of Business
   1015 Floyd Avenue
   Richmond, Virginia 23284
   (804) 257-1627

*National Center for World-of-Work Economic Education*
   Center for Economic Education
   North Texas State University
   Denton, Texas 76203
   (817) 788-2098

*National Depository for Economic Education Awards*
   Illinois State University
   Milner 184
   Normal, Illinois 61761
   (309) 436-3855-6

*National Center for Games and Simulation in Economic Education*
   Center for Economic Education
   University of Minnesota
   1169 Business Administration Building
   Minneapolis, Minnesota 55455
   (612) 307-4469

*National Center for Evaluation of High School Economics and Consumer Economics Textbooks and Supplemental Materials*
   Center for Economic Education
   California State University at Fullerton
   Fullerton, California 92631
   (714) 870-2248

Joint Council on Economic Education — **1212 Avenue of the Americas, New York, New York 10036 (212) 582-5150**

*GENERAL*
  Master Curriculum Guide for the Nation's Schools
    Part I Framework: Basic Concepts (No. 253)
    Part II Strategies for Teaching Economics
      Primary (No. 257)
      Intermediate (No. 258)
      Secondary
        Basic Business and Consumer Education (No. 259)
        U.S. History (No. 260)
        World Studies (No. 261)
  Learning Economics Through Children's Stories (No. 262)
  A Laboratory Approach to Economic Education (No. 227)
  Economics in History and the Social Sciences (No. 206)
  A Guide to Games and Simulations for Teaching Economics (No. 283)
  Economics in Social Studies Textbooks
    Book One - Elementary (No. 186)
    Book One Supplement
    Book Two - Junior High School (No. 187)
    Book Three - High School (No. 188)
    Book Four - History (No. 189)
    Set of four books
  Audiovisual Materials for Teaching Economics (No. 288)
  DEEP 1969: Perspectives on a 5-yr. Experiment in Curriculum Change (No. 118)
  Handbook for Curriculum change: Guildlines

*TESTS*
  Junior High School Test of Economics (Grades 7-9)
    Interpretive Manual and Rationale (No. 200)
    Package of 25 Re-usable Test Booklets (No. 201)
    Spanish Language test (No. 294)
  Primary Test of Economic Understanding (Grade 203)
    Examiner's Manual (No. 145)
    Package of 25 Re-usable Test Bookets (No. 146)
  Basic Economics Test (Grade 4-6)
    Examiner's Manual (No. 297)
    Test Booklets Package of 25 Form A (No. 295) Form B (No. 296)
    Discussion Guide and Rationale (No. 270)
    Test Booklets, package of 25 Form A (No. 268) Form B (No. 269)
    Test of Economic Literacy (Grade 11-12)
    Spanish Language Test. Form A (No. 292) Form B (No. 293)
  Revised Test of Understanding in College Economics (TUCE)
    Interpretive Manual (No. 307)
    Test Booklets package of 25 Macro: Form A (No 301) Form B No. 302)
                                  Micro: Form A (No. 303) Form B (No. 304)
                                  Macro/Micro: Form A (No. 305) Form B (No. 306)
  Test of Understanding in Personal Economics
    Manual and Discussion Guide (No. 132)
    Package of 25 Re-usable Test Booklets (No. 133)

*PERSONAL ECONOMICS*
  Teaching Personal Economics in the Social Studies Curriculum (No. 124)
  Teaching Personal Economics in the Home Economics Curriculum (No. 125)

Teaching Personal Economics in the Business Curriculum (No. 126)
Teaching a Course in Personal Economics (No. 127)

*Elementary School*
  Economics and Our Community (No. 185)
  The Child's World of Choices
    Teacher's Guide
    Student Activity Book
    (Order: Iowa Council on Economics Education
        University of Iowa, Iowa City, IA

*Junior High School*
  Government and the Economy (No. 204)

*Senior High School*
  Economics - Political Science Series
    Analyzing Crime and Crime Control (No. 267)
    Analyzing Tax Policy (No. 266)
    Analyzing Government Regulation (No. 265)
    Analyzing Health Care (No. 255)
    The Role of Unions in the American Economy (No. 230)
    Growth of the American Economy with Teacher's Guide (No. 160, 161)
    (Set of 25 plus TG)
    Economics in the Business Curriculum (No. 157)
    Teaching Economics in American History: A Systems Approach
      Teacher's Manual (No. 182)
      Color Slides (No. 198)
    Trade-off: The Land Use Planning Game (No. 276)

*University*
  Resource Manual for Teacher Training Programs in Economics (No. 271)
  Research in Teaching College Economics (No. 287)
  Alternative Approaches to the College Introductory Economics Course
      JEE Special Issue No. 1 (No. 209)
      JEE sSecial Issue No. 2 (No. 210)
      JEE Special Issue No. 3 (No. 211)
      JEE Special Issue No. 4 No. 212)
  Research Papers in Economic Education (No. 162)

  *The Journal of Economic Education*
    Back issues (Vol. 2, No. 2 through Vol 11, No. 2)
    Volume 12, No. 1, winter 1980 (No. 300)
    Volume 12, No. 2, Summer 1981

  *Economic Education Experiences*
    Back Issues (Vol. 10 through 17)
    Current Volume (No. 17 - No. 299) (No. 18 - No. 308)
    Among the Best (No. 291)

  *Economic Topics*
    The Economics of Youth Unemployment (No. 163)
    The Economic Role of Women (No. 252)
    The Economics of Professional Team Sports (No. 239)
    The Economics of Energy Problems (No. 223)
    The Economics of Health Care (No. 222)
    The Economics of Food Supply (No. 208)
    The Economics of Productivity/Teaching About (No. 191)

*Filmstrips and Visuals*

The Role of Unions in the American Economy (No. 242)
The Growth of the American Economy (No. 196)
The United States Economy in Action
    The Role of Consumers (No. 244)
    The Role of the Commercial Banking Systems (No. 246)
    Capital Investment (No. 229)
    The Role of the Federal Reserve System (No. 217)
The Economics of Business
    Business and Public Interest (No. 192)
    Economics and Business Enterprise (No. 193)
Economic Topics Series
    The Economics of Professional Team Sports (No. 223)
    The Economics of the Energy Problem (No. 234)
    The Economics of Health Care (No. 235)
    The Economics of Food Supply (No. 236)
    The Economics of Productivity (No. 237)
    The Economics of Youth Unemployment (No. 238)
Trade-offs
    Films - 16 mm. color and ¾" video cassettes
    Filmstrips - Sound cassettes
      Unit I - Decision - Making (No. 284)
      Unit II - Productivity (No. 285)
      Unit III - Buyers, Sellers, Markets (No. 286)
    Workshop leaders Handbook (No. 273)

The Big Rip-off: What Crime costs You (No. 277)
Health Care: Can You Afford to be sick? (No. 280)
Youth Unemployment: Causes and Consequences (No. 282)
Teaching Economics in American History (color slides) (No. 198)


## Resource Films

Free to Choose Film Series. Penn Communications, Inc. WQLN, Public Communications, Erie, Pa. 1980.
  The Power of the Market, The Tyranny of Control, Anatomy of a Crisis, From Cradle to Grave, Created Equal, What's Wrong With Our Schools?, Who Protects the Consumer?, Who Protects the Worker?, The Cure for Inflation, How to Stay Free.

Documentary for each film.